CONTEMPORARY'S
WRITING SKILLS
WORKBOOK SERIES

GED

BOOK 1
GRAMMAR & USAGE

By Nancy Kellman

Consulting Editor
Carol Nelson
Illinois Central College

Library of Congress Cataloging-in-Publication Data

Kellman, Nancy J.
    GED, the writing skills test.

    Contents: book 1. Grammar & usage—book 2.
Spelling, capitalization & punctuation—book 3.
Sentence structure, style & diction, and logic
& organization.
    1. English language—Examinations, questions,
etc.   2. General educational development tests—
Study guides.   I. Nelson, Carol.   II. Title.
PE1114.K4   1982   428'.0076   82-14476
ISBN 0-8092-5814-5 (v. 1)
ISBN 0-8092-5813-7 (v. 2)
ISBN 0-8092-5812-9 (v. 3)

Published by Contemporary Books, Inc.
180 North Michigan Avenue, Chicago, Illinois 60601
Manufactured in the United States of America
International Standard Book Number: 0-8092-5814-5

Published simultaneously in Canada by
Fitzhenry & Whiteside
91 Granton Drive
Richmond Hill, Ontario L4B 2N5
Canada

CONTENTS

VERB EXERCISES

SUBJECT AND VERB AGREEMENT EXERCISES

PRONOUN EXERCISES

ADJECTIVE AND ADVERB EXERCISES

FINAL SKILLS INVENTORY: GRAMMAR AND USAGE

TO THE LEARNER:

This workbook is designed to give you extra practice in one area of the GED Writing Skills Test—the grammar and usage portion. The other books in Contemporary's *GED Writing Skills Workbook Series* will help you prepare for the remaining areas of the Writing Skills Test.

HOW CAN THIS WORKBOOK
HELP YOU PREPARE FOR THE GED TEST?

Students taking the GED Test and teachers of GED preparation classes have commented that practice exercises are extremely important in scoring high on the test. Most GED preparation books do not offer enough practice exercises. Most of them only list rules and give only a few exercise items to show how these rules work.

The purpose of Contemporary's *GED Writing Skills Workbook Series,* however, is to offer plenty of practice exercises to strengthen your knowledge of this important area of the GED Test. Text and explanations are kept short to offer you the maximum amount of practice.

HOW SHOULD YOU USE
THE GRAMMAR AND USAGE WORKBOOK?

This extra-practice workbook is best used as you work through the grammar and usage section of Contemporary's main text *GED Test 1: The Writing Skills Test.* Doing the exercises as you use the main text will strengthen your skills and knowledge.

Skills Inventory and Evaluation Chart

A good way to start your work is by taking the **Skills Inventory.** There are 50 items to test your knowledge. Use the answers and explanations that follow the Skills Inventory to check your work. Finally, fill in the **Evaluation Chart** on page 4 to pinpoint the areas that might need special attention.

Practice Exercises, Text Pages, and Review Exercises

Each of the 44 **practice exercises** covers a topic that is presented in the grammar and usage section of the main text, Contemporary's *GED Test 1: The Writing Skills Test.* Many of the exercises start with a brief grammar and usage lesson. Read the explanations, examples, and directions that are given before you begin the exercise. If you have any trouble with the exercise, the **text pages** found in the margin will show you where to go for more information in the main text. **Review exercises** are included after each main topic to help you check your progress.

Text pages that are given in *italic type* correspond to editions printed for the 1988 GED tests. Text pages given in printed type correspond to the previous editions published between 1985 and 1987. To find out which edition you have, turn to the copyright page in the front of the text. Look for the year next to "copyright ©."

Final Skills Inventory and Evaluation Chart

Take the **Final Skills Inventory** after you have completed all 44 exercises in this workbook. Again, check your answers and fill in the **Evaluation Chart**.

All of the inventories, practice exercises, review exercises, answers and explanations, and charts can easily be torn out of this book. This was done so that you or your teacher can best decide how to use this book.

If you use this workbook for extra practice while you are studying the main text, you will be well-prepared to succeed on the GED Writing Skills Test.

Best wishes from Contemporary Books. We would enjoy hearing of your experiences as you use our materials to sharpen your knowledge of grammar and usage.

Skills Inventory: GRAMMAR AND USAGE

Directions: If one of the four underlined words or groups of words is an error in grammar or usage, blacken the space in the answer grid under the number corresponding to it. If there is no error, blacken the space numbered (5).

Example: *In most parts of the country, winter include snow, ice, and*
1   2   3

freezing temperatures.
4

1 2 **3** 4 5

1. Students often respects a teacher who is strict with them.
    1   3   4
    ②respect

    1. 1 2 3 4 5

2. Your going in the wrong direction according to my map.
    1   3   4
    ① you're 2

    2. 1 2 3 4 5

3. These kinds of boots are neither warm nor waterproof.
    1   2   3   ④

    3. 1 2 3 4 5

4. James wished he has more friends than he did.
    1   3   4
    ② had

    4. 1 2 3 4 5

5. The foods us Americans eat are different from those eaten in many
            1   2   3
    ① we

    other countries.
    4

    5. 1 2 3 4 5

6. Peanuts is a good, healthful snack because they are low in sugar.
            1   2   3   4
    ① are

    6. 1 2 3 4 5

7. Of all the musicals I have seen I enjoyed A Chorus Line more.
        1   2   3   4 most

    7. 1 2 3 4 5

8. The salespeople, Marv, Mel, and Laurie, all says that sales are lower
                        1   ② say   3 2

    this week than last.
            4

    8. 1 2 3 4 5

9. Nobody whom brings a donation will be turned away from the picnic.
            1 who 2   3   4

    9. 1 2 3 4 5

10. Who will decide to who we report if there is an emergency?
    1   2   ③ whom   4

    10. 1 2 3 4 5

11. Not only does the waitress serve tables, but also she clears it off.
    1   2   3 4   ④ them

    11. 1 2 3 4 5

12. This kind of meat tends to be tough and fatty.
    1   2   3   4

    12. 1 2 3 4 5

13. We volunteers worked long and patient at our jobs.
    1   ② 3   4   patiently
                   work

    13. 1 2 3 4 5

14. Hamburger is expensiver than eggs are.
                1 ② 3   4 more
                   expensive

    14. 1 2 3 4 5

15. The floors hear in the hospital must be cleaner for health's sake.
            ① here   2   3   4

    15. 1 2 3 4 5

16. Between you and I, today is the happiest day of my life.
            1 ② me   3   4
            me

    16. 1 2 3 4 5

17. Both of the movies at the theater were showed last week too.
    1   2   (3) shown 4

17. 1 2 3 4 5

18. Checkers and chess are popular games among both children and adults.
         1   2   3   4

18. 1 2 3 4 5

19. The man which works with me always talks to himself.
      (1) who 2   3   4

19. 1 2 3 4 5

20. Have you brung your check to be cashed?
      1 2 (3) brought 4

20. 1 2 3 4 5

21. Rae was real upset when the stain wouldn't come out of her dress.
          1 very 2 3 (really)   4

21. 1 2 3 4 5

22. Statistics show that much women work at full-time jobs out of their
            1   (2) most 3 many
homes as well as raise families.
        4

22. 1 2 3 4 5

23. Eva Peron never raised to vice-president of Argentina, although she
             (1) 2 rose   3
wanted the position badly.
              4

23. 1 2 3 4 5

24. A car with front-wheel drive handles well on ice and snow; it parks
        1   2   3
easy, too.
(4) easier (easily)

24. 1 2 3 4 5

25. The telephone ringing woke me from a sound sleep.
    (1)   2 3   4
    telephones

25. 1 2 3 4 5

26. The supervisor told us we must do our work more careful or we will be
             1 2   (3) carefully
fired.
 4

26. 1 2 3 4 5

27. Daniel is the boy which everyone wishes were his brother.
          (1) who 2   3   4

27. 1 2 3 4 5

28. Each of the team members deserves a medal because of their valiant
                   1   2
efforts in the game's final minutes.   (his or her)
  3   4

28. 1 2 3 4 5

29. Which is healthiest, plain yogurt or cottage cheese?
     1   2   (3) healthier 4

29. 1 2 3 4 5

30. Michael, who is my nephew, and his fiancée, Carla, make a wonderful
        1   2 3   4
couple.

30. 1 2 3 4 5

31. If Debbie felt so sickly, why didn't she stay home?
            1 (2) sick 3   4

31. 1 2 3 4 5

32. In the future there will be much chances to use computers in the home.
             1   2 3 (4) more many

32. 1 2 3 4 5

33. This class will teach me reading, writing and to spell.
    1   2   3   (4) spelling

33. 1 2 3 4 5

34. Jerry hurted his back badly while carrying the heavy boxes.
     (1) hurt   2   3   4

34. 1 2 3 4 5

35. These shoes are more tight than the ones I usually wear.
    1   (2) tighter 3   4

35. 1 2 3 4 5

36. <u>Whom</u> is <u>prettier</u>, Sharon or <u>I</u>?
   ①   2   3   4
  who

36.   1   2   3   4   5

37. Nobody can <u>run</u> the relay race <u>faster</u> than <u>you</u> and <u>I</u>.
           1   2   3   4

37.   1   2   3   4   5

38. Gert's constant <u>talking</u> along with her <u>husband</u> <u>falling</u> asleep made the
                1   2   ③ 4
                                   husband's
evening a disaster.

38.   1   2   3   4   5

39. All of <u>those</u> <u>radioes</u> are too <u>expensive</u> for <u>us</u> to consider.
         1   ② *radios;*   3   4

39.   1   2   3   4   5

40. Many <u>people</u> wish <u>they</u> could forget <u>they're</u> <u>pasts</u>.
        1   2   ③ 4
                           their

40.   1   2   3   4   5

41. File your tax forms <u>prompt</u> in order to <u>get</u> <u>your</u> refund <u>early</u>.
               ① *promptly* 2   3   4

41.   1   2   3   4   5

42. Some of the <u>tools</u> in the <u>cabinet</u> <u>is</u> in need of <u>cleaning</u> and oiling.
          1   2 ③ *are*   4

42.   1   2   3   4   5

43. Every <u>one</u> of the <u>students</u> <u>has</u> three <u>mouses</u> in his experiment.
      1   2   3   ④ *mouse's (mice)*

43.   1   2   3   4   5

44. Cross country <u>skiing</u> and <u>ice skate</u> are <u>popular</u> winter <u>sports</u>.
          1   ② *skating* 3   4

44.   1   2   3   4   5

45. Will <u>you</u> remind <u>everyone</u> to <u>bring</u> <u>their</u> donations for the rummage
    1   2   3   ④ *(his or her)*
sale?

45.   1   2   3   4   5

46. The new <u>employees</u> always <u>feel</u> <u>many</u> anxiety about <u>their</u> performance
          1   2 ③ *some (much)* 4 *the*
on the job.

46.   1   2   3   4   5

47. <u>Childrens'</u> pajamas must be fireproof, <u>although</u> <u>adults'</u> do not have to
   ①   2   3   4
be. *(children's)*

47.   1   2   3   4   5

48. The town looked <u>strangely</u> all <u>covered</u> with <u>deep</u> <u>white</u> snow.
         ① *strange* 2   3   4

48.   1   2   3   4   5

49. Gloria takes <u>her</u> aerobic <u>dance</u> routines <u>seriouser</u> than <u>I</u> take my
           1   2   ③   4
bookkeeping.   *more seriously*

49.   1   2   3   4   5

50. <u>Gently</u> and <u>quietly</u> the nurse turned the <u>sleeping</u> infant on <u>her</u> side.
    1   2   3   4

50.   1   2   3   4   5

−12/50

Answers and explanations begin on page 5.

SKILLS INVENTORY EVALUATION CHART

Directions: After completing the Skills Inventory, check your answers by using the Skills Inventory Answers and Explanations, pages 5-6. Write the total number of your *correct* answers for each skill area in the blank boxes below. If you have *more than one incorrect* answer in any skill area, you need more practice. Pages to study in your textbook (Contemporary's *GED Test 1: The Writing Skills Test*) are listed in the **Text Pages** column. To find out which edition of the text you have, turn to the copyright page in the front of the text. Look for the year next to "Copyright ©." Pages to study in this workbook (Contemporary's *Grammar and Usage*) are listed in the last column.

Skill Area	Item Numbers	Total	Number Correct	Text Pages (1985 editions)	Text Pages (1988, later ed.)	Workbook Pages
Plural Nouns	39, 43	2	___	34–37	45–47	18–20
Possessive Nouns	2, 25, 40, 47	4	___	37–38	48–50	22
Countable Nouns	22, 32, 46	3	1	39–40	*	23
Gerunds	33, 44	2	___	31	*	24–26
Verb Tense	4, 17, 20, 23, 34	5	___	70–87, 91–92	71–91	30–32
Subject-Verb Agreement	1, 6, 8, 42	4	1	97–118	92–104	35–40
Pronoun Case	5, 9, 10, 16, 36	5	1	48–59	50–55	43–46
Pronoun Number	11, 28, 45	3	3	60–62	201–203	47–48
Pronoun Person	19, 27	2	___	62–64	203–205	47–48
Adjective Form	31, 48	2	1	121–123	*	52
Adverb Form	13, 15, 21, 24, 26, 41	6	2	121–123	*	52
Adjective Comparison	14, 29, 34	3	___	126–130	*	57–60
Adverb Comparison	7, 49	2	1	126–130	*	57–60

Note: *A score of 32 or more correct is considered passing for this Inventory.*
*These topics are not directly tested on the 1988 and later versions of the GED Writing Skills Test.

Answers and Explanations: SKILLS INVENTORY

Directions: After completing the Skills Inventory (pages 1–3), use the Answers and Explanations to check your work. *On these pages,* circle the number of each item you correctly answered. Then turn to the Skills Inventory Evaluation Chart (page 4) and follow the directions given.

---

1. **(2)** The plural verb *respect* is needed because the subject *students* is plural.

2. **(1)** The contraction *You're* is needed; it means *You are. Your* is a possessive pronoun and cannot be the subject of the sentence.

3. **(5)** No error

4. **(2)** The past tense *had* is needed because the verb *wished* is in the past tense.

5. **(1)** The subjective pronoun *we* is needed.

6. **(1)** The plural verb *are* is needed because the subject *peanuts* is plural.

7. **(4)** *Most* is needed to show a comparison of more than two things.

8. **(2)** The plural verb *say* is needed because the subject *salespeople* is plural.

9. **(1)** The subjective pronoun *who* is needed.

10. **(3)** The objective pronoun *whom* is needed as the object of the preposition *to.*

11. **(4)** The plural pronoun *them* is needed because it refers to *tables,* which is plural.

12. **(5)** No error

13. **(4)** The adverb *patiently* is needed.

14. **(2)** The correct comparative adjective form is *more expensive.*

15. **(1)** *Here,* indicating a place, is correct in this sentence.

16. **(2)** The objective pronoun *me* is needed as the object of the preposition *between.*

17. **(3)** The correct past participle form of the verb is *shown.*

18. **(5)** No error

19. **(1)** The pronoun *who* should be used to refer to a person.

20. **(3)** The correct past participle form is *brought.*

21. **(1)** The adverb *really* is needed to modify the adjective *upset.*

22. **(2)** The adjective *many* is needed because *women* is a countable noun.

23. **(1)** The correct past form is *rose.*

24. **(4)** The adverb *easily* is needed to modify the verb *parks.*

(over)

25. **(1)** The possessive form *telephone's* is needed to explain whose ringing caused the problem.

26. **(3)** The adverb form *carefully* is needed.

27. **(1)** The pronoun *who* or *that* should be used to refer to a person.

28. **(2)** The singular pronoun *his* (or *her*) is needed because it refers to *each*, which is singular.

29. **(3)** The comparative form of the adjective *healthier* is needed because only two things are being compared.

30. **(5)** No error.

31. **(2)** The adjective form *sick* is needed after the linking verb *felt*.

32. **(4)** The adjective *many* is needed because *chances* is a countable noun.

33. **(4)** The gerund form *spelling* is needed as the direct object of the verb *will teach*.

34. **(1)** The correct past form is *hurt*.

35. **(2)** The correct comparative form is *tighter*.

36. **(1)** The subjective pronoun *Who* is needed.

37. **(5)** No error.

38. **(3)** The possessive form *husband's* is needed before the gerund *falling*.

39. **(2)** The correct plural of *radio* is *radios*.

40. **(3)** The correct possessive form is *their*. *They're* is a contraction which means *they are*.

41. **(1)** The adverb form *promptly* is needed.

42. **(3)** The plural verb *are* is needed because the subject *some* is plural.

43. **(4)** The correct plural of *mouse* is *mice*.

44. **(2)** The gerund form *ice skating* is needed as the subject of the sentence.

45. **(4)** The singular pronoun *his* (or *her*) is needed because it refers to *everyone*, which is singular.

46. **(3)** The adjective *much* or an expression such as *a great deal of* is needed because *anxiety* is not a countable noun.

47. **(1)** The correct possessive form of *children* is *children's*.

48. **(1)** The adjective form *strange* is needed. It is a predicate adjective describing the town.

49. **(3)** The correct comparative adverb form is *more seriously*.

50. **(5)** No error.

Complete the Skills Inventory Chart on page 4.

Exercise 1: DEFINING SENTENCES

A **sentence** consists of a **subject** and a **predicate** that communicate a complete thought. The part of a sentence that tells who or what the sentence is about is called the **simple subject**. The **simple predicate** tells what the subject does or is. Both parts of a sentence can have other words added to give more information about the simple subject and the simple predicate:

   Fred and Gloria are planning a trip downtown next weekend.
     Simple Subject = *Fred and Gloria* (who)
     Simple Predicate = *are planning* (what the subject is doing)

Text pages 30–32.
Text pages 20–24.

Directions: In each of the following sentences, underline the simple subject once and the simple predicate twice.

Example: *After Father's Day those <u>ties</u> <u>will be sold</u> for half price.*

1. My <u>dentist</u> <u>works</u> very slowly and carefully.
2. The <u>weight-lifters</u> <u>practiced</u> their breathing.
3. Food <u>prices</u> <u>have gone up</u> every month this year.
4. The elevator <u>operator</u> <u>has been</u> on strike for two days.
5. The day-care <u>center</u> <u>opens</u> at 8:00 a.m.
6. Gloria's widowed <u>mother</u> <u>is moving</u> in with her.
7. My <u>partner</u> <u>will deliver</u> the flowers at noon.
8. The new suntan <u>creams</u> <u>prevent</u> burning.
9. <u>David</u> <u>left</u> school after 10th grade.
10. Instead of macaroni, the <u>chef</u> <u>prepared</u> lasagna.
11. The <u>article</u> in the *Tribune* <u>moved</u> me to tears.
12. Surprisingly, the <u>judge</u> <u>declared</u> a mistrial in the child abuse case.
13. Fresh-squeezed orange <u>juice</u> <u>is</u> rich in Vitamin C.
14. The <u>runners</u> in the marathon <u>were pleased</u> with the cool weather.
          (were)
15. Some movie <u>reviewers</u> never <u>say anything</u> good about a new film.
        say

2/15

Answers begin on page 69.

Exercise 2: DETECTING SENTENCES I

A **sentence fragment** is not a complete sentence. It may lack either a subject or a predicate. A fragment may also be incomplete because it does not communicate a complete thought. You can test a group of words to see if it is a complete sentence by finding answers to these three questions:

   (1) *Who or what is this about?* (will tell you the subject)
   (2) *What about that?* (will tell you the predicate)
   (3) *What does this group of words say?* (will tell you if the words express a complete thought)

Text pages 32–33.
Text pages 24–25.

Directions: Use the three questions above to decide whether each group of words is a sentence or a fragment. Mark "S" for sentence or "F" for fragment in the blank at the right.

Example: *Got ink all over my hands.*   F

1. He chews only sugarless gum.   1. S
2. Puts her briefcase on her desk.   2. F
3. Everyone who came to the lecture.   3. F
4. Am looking for a road map of Texas.   4. F
5. The atlas is no help.   5. S
6. Air-conditioning uses a great deal of energy.   6. S
7. As the papers blew all about the room.   7. F
8. The minimum wage for part-time workers.   8. F
9. The gun control bill is not popular with this group.   9. S
10. Seeing the price of gold double within a week.   10. F
11. Just because he has a high school diploma.   11. F
12. The noise startled everyone.   12. S
13. Mount St. Helens, cause of so much concern in 1980.   13. F
14. The quartz watch runs on a tiny battery.   14. S
15. Taking care not to waste any time.   15. F
16. Only had instant coffee or tea.   16. F
17. Larry has taken the test four times now.   17. S
18. Without any improvement in his scores.   18. F
19. We must end runaway inflation!   19. S
20. Officials elected by the people in the district.   20. F

0/20

Answers begin on page 69.

Exercise 3: DETECTING SENTENCES II

Three types of sentences are more difficult to test for completeness:
1) The **command:** *Bring me some pie and coffee.*
   The simple subject *you* is understood.
   The simple predicate is *bring.*
2) The **question:** *What is the soup today?*
   The simple subject *soup* follows the simple predicate *is.*
3) The **exclamation:** *How weird!*
   The simple subject *it* and the simple predicate *is* are both
   understood.

types of sentences
command
question
exclamation

Text page 33.
Text pages 25–27.

Directions: In each of the following sentences, underline the simple subject
once and the simple predicate twice. If a subject or predicate is understood,
write it in parentheses after the sentence.

Example: *Open the door. (you)*

1. What a surprise the storm was!
2. Leave me alone. (you) S/U
3. Have you met the new tenants?
4. When will the alarm ring?
5. Where is the spare tire?
6. How lucky! S/U – P/U (it) (is)
7. Climb down the fire escape. S/U (you)
8. Why did Alex quit his job?
9. Bring me a bucket and a mop. S/U (you)
10. How graceful the young deer are.
11. Can anyone read the instructions on this package? S/U
12. Abandon ship! S/U (you)
13. How could the floor be so sticky?
14. What a hero you were!
15. Come along to the office with me. S/U (you)
16. Is Dad always so grumpy? S/U (My)
17. Never again will I visit this town!
18. What a dump! S/U (it) (is)
19. Don't speak to the newcomers yet. S/U (you)
20. Have you got the time, please?

–8/20

Answers begin on page 69.

Exercise 4:   FORMING SENTENCES

Directions: In the blank spaces below, write three of your own sentences that follow the pattern given. Your teacher will check your answers to be sure they are correct.

I. The Command

Example: *Be quiet in the assembly hall!*

1. You must be quiet in the assembly hall,
2. Quiet in the assembly hall,
3. The assembly hall must be quiet.

II. The Question

Example: *Haven't I seen you somewhere before?*

1. Have I seen you before?
2. I have seen you somewhere before, havent I?
3. I've seen you somewhere before

III. The Exclamation

Example: *What big eyes he has!*

1. You have big eyes
2. Big eyes are what you have
3. Your eyes are big

Exercise 5: REVIEW OF SENTENCES

Directions: If there is a sentence fragment in the following groups, blacken the space in the answer grid under the number corresponding to it. If all of the choices are complete sentences, blacken the space numbered (5).

Example:
   (1) *All the washing machines are being used.*
   (2) *Do you need some help?*
  (3) *And down the street, too.*
   (4) *What a bother he is!*

                                               1 2 **3** 4 5

1. (1) The flowers bloomed early.   **1.** 1 2 3 4 5
    (2) Will you look at that?
    (3) Larry has lost his car keys again.
    (4) Used hair spray instead of deodorant.

2. (1) Never studied when they were in school.   **2.** 1 2 3 4 5
    (2) Your tie is wild!
    (3) Richard lost nearly twenty pounds.
    (4) Whole wheat flour is brown.

3. (1) The apartment has been rented.   **3.** 1 2 3 4 5
    (2) Here are some messages for you.
    (3) Maria's English is improving.
    (4) Cicely Tyson is a fine actress.

4. (1) We ate in the non-smoking section.   **4.** 1 2 3 4 5
    (2) Wasn't an empty seat on the flight.
    (3) Clouds gathered before the storm.
    (4) That is just too expensive!

5. (1) An early morning walk along the lake.   **5.** 1 2 3 4 5
    (2) Who eloped?
    (3) Can someone translate this?
    (4) Maury and Gisella are Greek.

6. (1) The basic training camp is in Louisiana. **6.** 1 2 3 4 5
    (2) The garage roof is leaking.
    (3) Took a hot shower and felt better.
    (4) Those false nails look like claws!

7. (1) Jan always clips newspaper coupons.   **7.** 1 2 3 4 5
    (2) His children are living with his ex-wife.
    (3) The fire caused smoke damage.
    (4) Taco shells should be crisp, not soggy.

8. (1) People who buy on credit.   **8.** 1 2 3 4 5
    (2) I love Italian opera.
    (3) Isn't Bo Derek something?
    (4) The new highway will open next week.

(over)

9. (1) Melissa Manchester is fantastic!
   (2) After one year of work, you will have one week's vacation.
   (3) During the entire race for the gold medal.
   (4) Anyone who can operate a computer will be hired.

9. 1 2 3 4 5

10. (1) The programs on public television are educational.
    (2) The new Latino members of the school board.
    (3) Our furnace broke down.
    (4) The movers relaxed with cold beers.

10. 1 2 3 4 5

11. (1) What a close call!
    (2) Wash your hands.
    (3) Could have been a real expert.
    (4) Call me after dinner, please.

11. 1 2 3 4 5

12. (1) Are you sure?
    (2) Have you got a flashlight?
    (3) We won!
    (4) Where was the accident?

12. 1 2 3 4 5

13. (1) Lives in a dangerous time and place.
    (2) The beaches are closed.
    (3) What an unusual name!
    (4) I enjoy chocolate in any form.

13. 1 2 3 4 5

14. (1) The fans were thrilled.
    (2) Who will take their children?
    (3) Which type of heat does your building have?
    (4) From a tanker in the lake.

14. 1 2 3 4 5

15. (1) It is from a myth.
    (2) Even when I diet, I eat some chocolate.
    (3) Is that very American?
    (4) Look at all the crime reports!

15. 1 2 3 4 5

0/15

Answers begin on page 69.

Exercise 6: DEFINING NOUNS

A **noun** is a word that names a person, place, thing, or idea:
Melinda chose a new *backpack* from the *samples*.

Text pages 44-45.
Text pages 30-31.

Directions: In each of the following sentences, four words have been underlined. If one of the four words is a noun, blacken the space in the answer
grid under the number corresponding to it. If none of the four words is a
noun, blacken the space under number (5).

---

perso place thy

Example: John Bass owns his own plumbing company.
1 = noun, 2, 3, 4

1 2 3 4 5

1. The bus stopped at the corner near the new shopping
   center. verb / noun / adj / adj
   1. 1 (2) 3 4 5

2. When a husband and wife both work, they often share
   chores at home. adj / noun / verb / adj
   2. 1 (2) 3 4 5

3. If the bus drivers go on strike, I will have to get to my job
   another way. noun / verb / pronoun / adj
   3. (1) 2 3 4 5

4. Have you noticed how violent most cartoons are?
   verb / adj / noun / verb
   4. 1 2 (3) 4 5

5. Today's newspaper predicts higher taxes in the future
   instead of lower ones. noun / adj / adj / adj
   5. (1) 2 3 4 5

6. The pictures from Nancy's thirty-fifth birthday party were
   wonderful. noun / adj / verb / adj
   6. (1) 2 3 4 5

7. Evelyn is starting another new diet, but we know she
   won't stay on it. verb / noun / conj
   7. 1 2 (3) 4 5

8. Some high schools offer classes that teach students how to
   practice self-defense. verb / verb
   8. 1 2 3 4 (5)

9. Dr. Romero told me to come to the hospital for more
   tests. noun / verb / adj
   9. (1) 2 3 4 5

10. I wonder if it is wise to marry young; maybe we would
    have fewer divorces if people waited longer to marry.
    10. 1 2 3 (4) 5

0/10

Answers begin on page 69.

Exercise 7: USING NOUNS I

A noun can be used in several different ways in a sentence.

1) One use of nouns is as the **simple subject** of the sentence:
   Reggie drives the afternoon bus route.
2) A second use of nouns is as a **predicate nominative.** A predicate nominative renames or identifies the subject in the predicate part of the sentence:
   The champion was *Jack Johnson.*

Note: Predicate nominatives usually follow forms of the verb *to be* (*is, was, are,* etc.) or forms of the verbs *to become, to appear,* etc.

Text pages 44-45.
Text page 32.

Directions: Underline the noun used as the simple subject of each sentence below. Circle any nouns used as predicate nominatives.

Example: *Louis is an extremely active child.*

1. Our class meets in room 311.
2. Colleen is an excellent typist.
3. Liza Minelli became a star as a teenager.
4. The preacher of our church is a woman.
5. Some soldiers will become heroes for their brave actions.
6. The deadline for submitting refund requests was Tuesday.
7. Goldie lives way out in the country.
8. The worst problem at the ball game was the mosquitoes.
9. A penny saved is a penny earned.
10. The smoke detector saved our lives!
11. The movie was a French comedy.
12. Janice is the best cook in our family.
13. The college opens after Labor Day.
14. The spice in the sauce was ginger.
15. People become experts after taking this class.
16. The dogs are hunters.
17. Greta was a wonderful actress.
18. Sharla set the stove at 350°.
19. This cold weather is a surprise.
20. The only sound was the wind.

Answers begin on page 69.

Exercise 8: USING NOUNS II

3) A noun can be used as an **appositive**—a noun which immediately follows another noun and labels or gives additional information about the first noun:

   Skipper, our *parakeet*, cheers up our apartment.

4) A noun can be used as an **object of a preposition** by following a connecting word like *for, to, on, up, in, at, under, through, of,* etc:

   The leftovers are in the *refrigerator*.

Text pages 32-33.

Directions: Underline each noun used as an appositive in the sentences below. Circle each noun used as an object of a preposition.

Example: *Sari, my best friend, knits sweaters for the entire family.*

1. The car, a hatchback, has plenty of room for packages.
2. The lights in the basement are on a separate switch from the ones in the rest of the house.
3. How can Archie's wife Edith stand his put-downs?
4. The flood, a freak of nature, destroyed the entire valley.
5. Through the screens came the tiny flies, unwelcome guests at our gathering.
6. Tom Drewes, president of the company, just retired.
7. The pilot lights on the stove have gone out.
8. The mayor of the city, Jane Byrne, is planning another outdoor music festival on the lakefront.
9. Edward Kennedy, Senator from Massachusetts, may run for the presidency in the future.
10. Lobster tail, an expensive food, is not even on the menu in many restaurants.
11. Debbie, my niece, has a cold.
12. The pens in the drawer are for the cashier.
13. Does your cat Apollo wake you in the morning?
14. Under the dresser is the shoe.
15. The novel, *Madame Bovary*, is a work of art.

9/15

Answers begin on page 69.

Exercise 9:   USING NOUNS III

5) A noun can be used as a **direct object**. A direct object is the person, place, or thing that receives the action of the verb:
   The farmers plowed their *fields*.

6) A noun can be used as an **indirect object**. An indirect object is the noun which names the person, place, or thing *to* whom or *for* whom the action of the verb is done:
   The inspector gave the *landlord* a warning.
   Warning is the direct object of the sentence.

Note: The indirect object never follows the word *to* or *for*:
   Jeanette brought a gift for *Barbara*.
   (*Barbara* is the object of the preposition *for*.)
   Jeanette brought *Barbara* a gift.
   (*Barbara* is the indirect object.)

Text pages 32–33.

Directions: Underline each noun used as a direct object in the sentences below. Circle any noun used as an indirect object in the sentences below.

Example: *The judge gave the (jury) its instructions.*

1. The boss told his secretary a dirty joke.
2. Everyone brought Betsy flowers in the hospital.
3. A special bus drives the senior citizens to the class.
4. The heat wave may cause riots.
5. The clerk gave the happy customer the beautifully wrapped package.
6. We picked the strawberries late in June.
7. Julia Child taught her audience the trick of making smooth gravy.
8. The guard dog barked his warning.
9. Howard loaned Jerry a ladder to clean his gutters.
10. That class teaches people karate.
11. The bar will not serve minors liquor.
12. He bought candy for his girlfriend.
13. Everyone admires Rose Kennedy's courage.
14. The owner gave the boys a discount.
15. We give local stores our business.

Exercise 10: REVIEW OF NOUN USES

Directions: Six ways that nouns can be used are listed below. In each sentence, one noun has been underlined. Write the number of its correct use in the blank at the right.

USES OF NOUNS

1—Simple Subject   4—Predicate Nominative
2—Appositive   5—Object of a Preposition
3—Direct Object   6—Indirect Object

Example: *That story is a classic.*   4

1. <u>Exercise</u> is extremely important for good health. ①   1
2. Gerry wanted the <u>job</u> that was just filled. ②   3
3. The police officer read the arrested <u>man</u> his rights. ③   6
4. Should a secretary have to make coffee for the <u>boss</u>? ④   6 ✗ 5
5. The pink flowers are <u>carnations</u>. ⑤   2 ✗ 4
6. Isabel, the <u>librarian</u>, reads a book a week. ⑥   4 ✗ 2
7. Irving Wallace, my favorite <u>author</u>, has written another best-seller. ⑦   4 ✗ 2
8. That strange odor must be <u>ammonia</u>. ⑧   3 ✗ 4
9. Eating taffy always hurts my <u>teeth</u>. ⑨   6 ✗ 3
10. A policeman gave the <u>gang</u> a second chance to clean up their turf. ⑩   6
11. We will meet at <u>McDonald's</u> at noon. ⑪   5
12. The announcer is <u>Howard Cosell</u>. ⑫   4
13. A <u>strike</u> has ended the train service to and from the city. ⑬   1
14. John Davidson, <u>host</u> of his own show, sings as well as conducts interviews. ⑭   4 ✗ 2
15. A good diet <u>for</u> serious <u>athletes</u> contains plenty of protein. ⑮   6 ✗ 5
16. The Southwest is mostly <u>desert</u>. ⑯   ✗ 4
17. A burglar took the <u>jewelry</u> from the safe. ⑰   3
18. John gave <u>Cathy</u> a ride on his motorcycle. ⑱   6
19. Ground beef is on sale at the <u>supermarket</u> today. ⑲   5
20. Can <u>records</u> be checked out of the public library? ⑳   1

9/20

Answers begin on page 70.

Exercise 11: FORMING PLURALS I

There are many rules for forming **plurals** of nouns. The word plural means *more than one:*
Many *books* were sold at the fair.

1) The plural of most nouns is formed by simply adding *s:*
    car, cars
2) The plural of nouns ending with an *s, sh, ch, x,* or *z* is formed by adding *es:*
    brush, brushes
3) The plural of hyphenated nouns is formed by adding *s* to the main noun:
    father-in-law, fathers-in-law; vice-president, vice-presidents
4) The plural of nouns ending with *ful* is formed by adding *s* at the end of the word:
    spoonful, spoonfuls

Text pages 45–47.
Text pages 34–35.

Directions: If there is an incorrect plural form in the following groups of nouns, blacken the space in the answer grid under the number corresponding to it. If all of the plurals are correct, blacken the space numbered (5).

Example: *(1) ducks (2) wishes (3) catches (4) crashs*

1	2	3	4	5

1. (1) eagles (2) thrushes (3) parrots (4) finches

2. (1) sisters-in-law (2) half-brothers (3) attorney-at-laws (4) masters-of-ceremonies

3. (1) watches (2) bracelets (3) necklaces (4) crowns

4. (1) mouthfuls (2) bagsful (3) handfuls (4) drawerfuls

5. (1) riches (2) hopes (3) kisses (4) witchs

6. (1) cousins-to-be (2) buzzes (3) teaspoonsful (4) great-aunts

7. (1) blazes (2) dashes (3) blotches (4) axes

8. (1) half-sisters (2) brother-in-laws (3) pocketfuls (4) crutches

9. (1) reflexes (2) boxes (3) arches (4) gashes

10. (1) batches (2) latches (3) matches (4) slackes

Answer grid numbered 1 through 10, each with columns 1 2 3 4 5.

4/10

Answers begin on page 70.

Exercise 12:   FORMING PLURALS II

Here are more rules for forming the plurals of nouns.

5) The plural of nouns that end with a *y* is formed by adding *s* if the *y* follows a vowel *(a,e,i,o,u)*:
   valley, valleys; day, days

6) The plural of nouns that end with a *y* is formed by changing the *y* to an *i* and adding *es* if the *y* follows a consonant:
   baby, babies; berry, berries

7) The plural of nouns that end with an *o* is formed by adding *s* if the *o* follows another vowel:
   stereo, stereos

8) The plural of nouns that end with an *o* is usually formed by adding *es* if the *o* follows a consonant:
   tomato, tomatoes; hero, heroes

There are many exceptions to rule 8, especially with terms relating to music. You will need to check a dictionary for plurals such as *piano, pianos* and *soprano, sopranos*.

Text pages 45-47.
Text page 35.

Directions: If there is an incorrect plural form in the following groups of nouns, blacken the space under the number corresponding to it. If all of the plurals are correct blacken the space numbered (5).

Example: *(1) videos   (2) skys   (3) gulleys   (4) turkeys*

		1	2	3	4	5
Example		1	**2**	3	4	5
1.	(1) funnies (2) potatoes (3) plays (4) joys	1	2	3	4	5
2.	(1) delays (2) pennys (3) keys (4) stories	1	2	3	4	5
3.	(1) buggies (2) candies (3) bluejays (4) blueberrys	1	2	3	4	5
4.	(1) lilys (2) rays (3) flies (4) rodeos	1	2	3	4	5
5.	(1) echoes (2) secretaries (3) autos (4) mysteries	1	2	3	4	5
6.	(1) radios (2) torpedoes (3) librarys (4) studios	1	2	3	4	5
7.	(1) tomatoes (2) relays (3) toys (4) ponys	1	2	3	4	5
8.	(1) altos (2) holidays (3) cellos (4) monkeys	1	2	3	4	5
9.	(1) butterflies (2) french frys (3) photos (4) donkeys	1	2	3	4	5
10.	(1) trolleys (2) candies (3) pianos (4) avocados	1	2	3	4	5
11.	(1) turkeys (2) studies (3) puppys (4) cavities	1	2	3	4	5
12.	(1) banjoes (2) directories (3) mysteries (4) potatoes	1	2	3	4	5
13.	(1) echoes (2) burros (3) sopranos (4) ladies	1	2	3	4	5

Answers begin on page 70.

Exercise 13:   FORMING PLURALS III

The rules for the groups of nouns below have many exceptions. Check the dictionary when forming plurals for these groups of nouns. Here are a few general rules:

9)   The plural of nouns ending with an *f* or *fe* is sometimes formed by adding *s;* sometimes it is formed by changing the *f* or *fe* to *v* and adding *es:*

   roof, roofs; thief, thieves; knife, knives

10)   The plural of some nouns is the same as the singular:

   one fish, two fish; one deer, two deer

11)   Some nouns can be used only in the plural form:

   trousers; scissors

12)   The plural of some nouns is formed by changing the spelling:

   tooth, teeth; mouse, mice

13)   The plural of nouns ending with *man* or *woman* is formed by making the same spelling change you would make if you were forming the plural of *man* or *woman* alone:

   salesman, salesmen; superwoman, superwomen

14)   The plural of some nouns ending with *is* is formed by changing the *is* to *es:*

   hypothesis, hypotheses; basis, bases

15)   Many nouns have been borrowed from other languages. The plural of these nouns is formed according to rules of the language from which they were borrowed. You must memorize the correct plural forms of these words:

   datum, data; memorandum, memoranda; etc.

Text pages 45-47.
Text page 36.

Directions: If there is an incorrect plural form in the following groups of nouns, blacken the space in the answer grid under the number corresponding to it. If there is no error, blacken the space numbered (5).

Example: *(1) cuffs (2) loaves (3) fishs (4) parentheses*

	1	2	3	4	5
			▮		

1.   (1) mice   (2) trout   (3) staffs   (4) halves

2.   (1) children   (2) repairmen   (3) crises   (4) knives

3.   (1) alumni   (2) memorandums   (3) moose   (4) eyeglasses

4.   (1) policemans   (2) wives   (3) bases   (4) feet

5.   (1) lifes   (2) cattle   (3) scissors   (4) data

6.   (1) clothes   (2) underwears   (3) pants   (4) trousers

7.   (1) cliffs   (2) beliefs   (3) thiefs   (4) puffs

8.   (1) servicewomen   (2) lice   (3) bluffs   (4) furnitures

	1	2	3	4	5
1.	1	2	3	4	5
2.	1	2	3	4	5
3.	1	2	3	4	5
4.	1	2	3	4	5
5.	1	2	3	4	5
6.	1	2	3	4	5
7.	1	2	3	4	5
8.	1	2	3	4	5

Answers begin on page 70.

Exercise 14: FORMING PLURALS REVIEW

Directions: If there is an incorrect plural form in the following groups of nouns, blacken the space in the answer grid under the number corresponding to it. If there is no error, blacken the space numbered (5).

Example: *(1) nails (2) polishes (3) brushes (4) handsful*   1 2 3 **4** 5

1. (1) children (2) places (3) citys (4) pails   1. 1 2 3 4 5

2. (1) churches (2) pens (3) fishs (4) lines   2. 1 2 3 4 5

3. (1) women (2) ladies (3) men (4) boys   3. 1 2 3 4 5

4. (1) mice (2) crisises (3) glasses (4) tomatoes   4. 1 2 3 4 5

5. (1) stereos (2) pianoes (3) monkeys (4) cupfuls   5. 1 2 3 4 5

6. (1) brushes (2) switches (3) brother-in-laws (4) valleys   6. 1 2 3 4 5

7. (1) babies (2) skies (3) days (4) branches   7. 1 2 3 4 5

8. (1) deer (2) moose (3) teeth (4) sheeps   8. 1 2 3 4 5

9. (1) toys (2) stories (3) beliefs (4) data   9. 1 2 3 4 5

10. (1) historys (2) plays (3) solos (4) alumnae   10. 1 2 3 4 5

11. (1) waitresses (2) checks (3) windowswasher (4) caddies   11. 1 2 3 4 5

12. (1) echoes (2) chiefs (3) potatoes (4) firemens   12. 1 2 3 4 5

13. (1) cries (2) laughes (3) hiccups (4) frowns   13. 1 2 3 4 5

14. (1) measles (2) sneezes (3) basises (4) prices   14. 1 2 3 4 5

15. (1) clutchs (2) wheels (3) lights (4) horns   15. 1 2 3 4 5

16. (1) daisies (2) replayes (3) sons-in-law (4) prizes   16. 1 2 3 4 5

17. (1) matches (2) pajamas (3) scissors (4) parties   17. 1 2 3 4 5

18. (1) sudses (2) taxis (3) moose (4) feet   18. 1 2 3 4 5

19. (1) roofs (2) hoofs (3) cellos (4) flashes   19. 1 2 3 4 5

20. (1) relatives (2) grandparents (3) sisters-in-law (4) nephews   20. 1 2 3 4 5

Answers begin on page 70.

Exercise 15: FORMING THE POSSESSIVE

The **possessive** form of a noun shows ownership or relationship:
Peter's jacket is down-filled.

Follow the three rules below when forming possessives:

1) The possessive of singular nouns is formed by adding *'s*. Even when a singular noun ends in *s*, add *'s* to form the possessive:
   Mr. *Liss's* car; the *girl's* address
2) The possessive of plural nouns ending with an *s* is formed by adding only the apostrophe:
   four *hours'* sleep
3) The possessive of plural nouns that do not end with an *s* is formed by adding *'s*:
   men's locker room

Text pages 48–50.
Text pages 37–38.

Directions: Each underlined noun in the following sentences has been made possessive. If the possessive is used and spelled correctly, write "correct" on the blank after the sentence. If the underlined word is not correctly used or spelled, write the corrected word on the blank.

Example: *The sinks' drain is clogged.*   *sinks*

1. Did the children's mother just leave them? _____
2. That bus' windows are all steamed up. _____
3. My landlords rules are ridiculous. _____
4. All of the miner's wives waited for their safe return. _____
5. Steve is taking two week's vacation. _____
6. Have you had your cat's claws removed? _____
7. The protester's complaints never reached the mayor. _____
8. Dr. Jones' office is in the new medical center. _____
9. This glass's rim is chipped. _____
10. The peoples' choice seems to be to keep the schools open. _____
11. The sandwiches' fillings were tuna and egg salad. _____
12. This battery's charge is getting weak. _____
13. Have city worker's jobs been cut? _____
14. Mr. Gross' family all respect him. _____
15. Gloria Steinem fights for women's rights. _____

Answers begin on page 70.

Exercise 16:   AVOIDING PROBLEMS WITH NOUNS

When using nouns, pay special attention to these problem areas.

1) **Uncountable nouns,** such as *knowledge, time,* and *equipment,* do not have a plural form. Words that describe an uncountable noun must identify the quantity without using specific numbers:
   A large amount of money was stolen.
   See page 36 in Contemporary's *GED Test 1: The Writing Skills Test* for a list of words that can be used with uncountable nouns.
2) When you use *kind of, type of,* or *sort of,* do not use *a* or *an* before the noun:
   That *kind of* plant makes me sneeze.
3) *Kind of, type of,* or *sort of* must agree in number with the nouns they refer to:
   That *type of* doughnut is very greasy.
   (singular)
   Two *kinds of* people came—the curious ones and the helpful ones.
   (plural)

Text pages 39-41.

Directions: Correct the underlined part of the following sentences. Write the corrected sentence in the space. If there is no error in the sentence, write "correct" in the space.

Example: *I like these kind of* apple. *I like this kind of apple.*

1. This kind of onions taste sweet.

2. After these sorts of accidents, blood donors are always needed.

3. How much problems can one family have?

4. The boss assigned a large number of work to me.

5. That type of a child is fun to be around.

6. Can this type of holes be plugged up?

7. Those kinds of insect don't sting.

Exercise 17: RECOGNIZING GERUNDS

Gerunds are special kinds of nouns. They are formed from verbs but are always used as nouns. Gerunds always end in *ing*:
  talking (to talk); *driving* (to drive)

Gerunds may be used in any of the ways a noun can be used:
  Saying goodbye was painful. (simple subject)
  We enjoy *skating*. (direct object)
  My talent, *singing*, is my hobby and my job. (appositive)
  The students cannot learn without *studying*. (object of a preposition)
  One of the most popular winter sports is cross-country *skiing*. (predicate nominative)

Text page 31.

Directions: Underline the gerund(s) in each sentence below. On the blank after the sentence, tell how the gerund is used.

Example: *Saving money is very difficult these days.* *simple subject*

1. You will learn most by practicing. _____
2. Speaking in front of a group makes me nervous. _____
3. Jack teaches accounting at night school. _____
4. Tampering with a mailbox is a felony. _____
5. Our family's favorite vacation is hiking in the country. _____
6. You will get a ticket for parking there. _____
7. Drinking and driving are a hazardous combination. _____
8. You must stop that shouting! _____
9. Bernie's hobby, golfing, allows him to relax after a hard day at work. _____
10. Have you tried folk dancing? _____
11. Do you like ironing? _____
12. Burping a baby is very important. _____
13. It prevents spitting up and gas pains. _____
14. Gena's job, bookkeeping, requires careful concentration. _____
15. You will be fired for embezzling that money. _____

Answers begin on page 70.

Exercise 18:   USING GERUNDS CORRECTLY

When a gerund is used with another noun, the possessive of the other noun must be used to show the relationship between the two words:
   The *family's* arguing is getting worse.

Text pages 37-38.

Directions: If there is an error in one of the following sentences, write the corrected sentence in the space provided. If there is no error in a sentence, write "correct" in the space.

Example: *Judi cracking her gum annoys me.*
   Judi's cracking her gum annoys me.

1. Jose fixing his car made a lot of noise.

2. David walking in the snow left deep tracks.

3. That company's printing is expensive, but excellent.

4. The children laughing brightened my mood.

5. Make room on the table for Grandma sewing.

6. Dad cooking is a joke.

7. Everyone complained about Marie washing the floor with a dirty mop.

8. We listened carefully to the coach calling the plays.

9. The boat rocking makes many people feel ill.

10. I wish someone could stop the baby crying.

11. The television playing so loud distracts me.

12. You salting your food is not healthy.

(over)

13. A person dreaming tells a lot about him._____
_____

14. Donna's gunning the motor wastes gas._____
_____

15. The shutter flapping frightened the children._____
_____

16. Debbie calling me made me lose my train of thought._____
_____

17. Willie playing the drums always attracts an audience._____
_____

18. You cutting your own hair was a disaster!_____
_____

19. Me wearing new shoes usually means blisters on my feet._____
_____

20. Ellen drinking coffee keeps her awake at night._____
_____

Answers begin on page 71.

Exercise 19:   NOUN REVIEW

Directions: In each of the following sentences, four words or groups of words have been underlined. If one of these words is an error, blacken the space in the answer grid under the number corresponding to it. If there is no error in the sentence, blacken the space under number (5).

Example: *We caught a large <u>number</u> of <u>fishes</u> due to*
                                        1   2
<u>Raymond's</u> bringing the right <u>kind of</u> bait.
       3   4

```
1  2  3  4  5
```

1. The <u>doorbell</u> ringing while I am taking a <u>bath</u>—that is the
          1   2
    <u>type of</u> <u>disturbance</u> I hate.
       3   4

    1.   1 2 3 4 5

2. <u>Too many</u> <u>furniture</u> makes the <u>room's</u> <u>walls</u> seem to close
        1   2   3   4
    in.

    2.   1 2 3 4 5

3. <u>John McEnroe's</u> tennis <u>playing</u> was good, but his
           1   2
    <u>outbursts</u> disturbed his <u>opponent's</u> concentration.
        3   4

    3.   1 2 3 4 5

4. <u>Scissors</u>, paper, and <u>glue</u> were the <u>supplys</u> for the <u>class's</u>
        1   2   3   4
    art project.

    4.   1 2 3 4 5

5. <u>Jerry's</u> banging on the <u>pianoes</u> <u>keys</u> gave me one of
        1   2   3
    <u>those kinds of</u> headaches.
            4

    5.   1 2 3 4 5

6. The <u>pencils</u> <u>points</u> are too dull for drawing <u>that kind of</u>
            1   2   3
    <u>blueprint</u>.
        4

    6.   1 2 3 4 5

7. Healthy <u>people's</u> <u>hairs</u> and <u>nails</u> are always growing and
               1   2   3
    replacing themselves, but <u>teeth</u> cannot do this.
                                  4

    7.   1 2 3 4 5

8. White blood <u>cells</u> <u>function</u> is fighting <u>disease</u> and helping
                   1   2   3
    <u>bodies</u> stay healthy.
        4

    8.   1 2 3 4 5

9. The <u>women's</u> <u>bathroom's</u> <u>doors</u> were locked by the
            1   2   3
    <u>building's</u> owner.
        4

    9.   1 2 3 4 5

10. <u>Today's</u> <u>news</u> told of <u>Israel's</u> <u>attackes</u> on Arab oil fields.
        1   2   3   4

    10. 1 2 3 4 5

(over)

11. Doris' birthday presents were from her sisters-in-law and
    1   2   3
    half-brothers.
    4
    11. 1 2 3 4 5

12. Some of the machineries was damaged by Sunday's storm,
    1   2
    but it can't be repaired until Monday.
    3   4
    12. 1 2 3 4 5

13. Bruce's girlfriend stayed at her mothers' house when she
    1   2
    caught the children's measles.
    3   4
    13. 1 2 3 4 5

14. Nancy's typing is terrible; Gloria's is much faster because
    1   2   3
    her equipments is newer.
    4
    14. 1 2 3 4 5

15. These kinds of bikes need special wrenchs to adjust their
    1   2
    brakes and gears.
    3   4
    15. 1 2 3 4 5

16. John washing the clothes in hot water was a mistake.
    1   2   3   4
    16. 1 2 3 4 5

17. Bluejays, beautiful birds to look at, are vicious enemys to
    1   2   3
    many gentler species of birds.
    4
    17. 1 2 3 4 5

18. Rubies, emeralds, diamonds—all the jeweleries had been
    1   2   3   4
    stolen.
    18. 1 2 3 4 5

19. These kinds of shoes with leather soles feel best on my
    1   2   3
    feet.
    4
    19. 1 2 3 4 5

20. Some family arguing at the dinner table can cause ulcers.
    1   2   3   4
    20. 1 2 3 4 5

21. The child's problem is a result of his two parent's
    1   2   3   4
    permissiveness.
    21. 1 2 3 4 5

22. Todays weather makes children want to run on the beach.
    1   2   3   4
    22. 1 2 3 4 5

23. Toyotas and Datsuns are those kind of imports that cut
    1   2   3   4
    down on the sale of American cars.
    23. 1 2 3 4 5

24. Some instructors' class's are interesting, but others' are
    1   2   3
    duller than sermons.
    4
    24. 1 2 3 4 5

25. The boys' drinking alcohols is a serious problem.
    1   2   3   4
    25. 1 2 3 4 5

Answers begin on page 71.

Exercise 20:   IDENTIFYING VERBS

A **verb** is a word or group of words that shows action. A verb helps to make a sentence by linking the subject to a word or idea that describes the subject. Verb tenses set the sentence in a time period:
  We *have eaten* at the restaurant many times.

Text page 71.
Text pages 71-72.

Directions: Underline the verbs in the sentences below. Be sure to underline all the parts of the verb and all the verbs in each sentence.

Example: *Sofia has often traveled from Poland to the United States.*

1. Alonzo stirred the onions and garlic together.
2. Janice will be your new supervisor.
3. Has anyone reported the accident to the police?
4. If the ladder slips, you will break your neck!
5. Martina Navratilova became a citizen of the United States in 1981.
6. Your vote will decide the election.
7. Dana left early because she felt ill.
8. Wisconsin is called "America's Dairyland."
9. Most mystery novels give clues throughout the story.
10. When the lights dimmed, the crowd booed.
11. Joey can sleep in any bed, but his sister Gayle needs her own bed and pillow.
12. When factories pour hot liquids into streams or lakes, they cause thermal pollution.
13. There is no cure for the common cold, but aspirin relieves some of the discomfort.
14. The driver behind us saw us, but still hit the back end of our car.
15. Every time the door slams, Mattie jumps.
16. Lucille Ball has always been my favorite comedienne.
17. We spread the blanket for our picnic.
18. I must write to my mother-in-law tonight!
19. During the storm, our power lines snapped.
20. The record has been a hit for months.

Answers begin on page 71.

Exercise 21:   FORMING VERB TENSES

Present, past, and **future** are the three basic verb tenses. Some verbs form their past tense in a regular manner, by adding *ed:*
  look, looked; pick, picked; rain, rained; jump, jumped

Some verbs, called **irregular verbs,** form their past tense differently:
  bring, brought; eat, ate; come, came; sing, sang

To be certain of the correct past tense form of any verb, you can check the dictionary.

Text pages 72-75.
Text pages 72-83.

Directions: Underline the correct past tense of each verb in parentheses.

Example: *No one (weared, <u>wore</u>) a warm jacket.*

1.   Ryan (throwed, threw) the ball to the plate.
2.   I (wrote, writ) a seven-page letter to Carlow.
3.   The class (understanded, understood) the assignment.
4.   When it got dark, we all (ran, run) home.
5.   Gilda (slept, sleeped) until past noon.
6.   The mail workers (striked, struck) for higher pay.
7.   The boxers (fought, fighted) only six rounds.
8.   Yesterday, Diana Nyad (swum, swam) across the bay.
9.   Lou (catched, caught) a cold on his camping trip.
10.   The bird (flew, flied) over the rainbow.
11.   Someone just (stoled, stole) a car from the parking lot.
12.   The crowd (been, was) at the race since early afternoon.
13.   The announcer (sayed, said) the show would go on.
14.   Leonard and Doris (losed, lost) everything in the fire.
15.   I sure (feeled, felt) awful about their bad luck.
16.   Gayle (bit, bited) into the corn eagerly.
17.   Everyone (saw, seen) the fireworks.
18.   I never (ate, eaten) such spicy food!
19.   Who (taked, took) all of the change?
20.   Ms. Johnson (teached, taught) math to the first graders.

Answers begin on page 71.

Exercise 22: USING VERB TENSES CORRECTLY

In addition to the present, past, and future tenses of regular and irregular verbs, there are four additional, more complicated tenses a verb can take.

Text pages 76-90.
Text pages 83-87.

Directions: Before each sentence below, the infinitive form of the verb is written in parentheses. Decide on the correct form of the verb needed to fill in the blank in the sentence. Write the correct verb form in the blank.

Example: *(to bring) Cissie* _brought_ *her boys to the class.*

1. (to eat) Have you _____ yet?

2. (to see) Everyone had _____ the movie.

3. (to go) When will you _____ to Washington?

4. (to write) Davida _____ a letter to her boyfriend yesterday.

5. (to write) Have you _____ down your Social Security number?

6. (to light) A minute ago Mark _____ a match so we could see.

7. (to feel) I've never _____ so sick before.

8. (to speak) Has the main character _____ yet?

9. (to hurt) Ms. Miller just _____ herself on the rough edges of the desk.

10. (to hear) We haven't _____ from the unemployment office.

11. (to get) Has Steve _____ his raise yet?

12. (to break) How could the new car have _____ down already?

13. (to sleep) Barry _____ on the sofa in the living room last night.

14. (to leave) When my family _____, I felt very lonely.

15. (to freeze) The popsicles haven't _____ yet.

16. (to wash) Tomorrow I must _____ my hair.

(over)

17. (to drink)   The baby usually _____ a bottle of formula every four hours.

18. (to sweep)   Don _____ the floor before his in-laws arrived.

19. (to know)   If I had _____ how late it was, I'd have stayed at home.

20. (to think)   Freddi promises she will _____ about our offer.

21. (to slip)   Everyone _____ on that loose rug by the door as he comes in.

22. (to buy)   We had _____ new drapes, but they looked so awful we returned them.

23. (to answer)   The operator is _____ your call now.

24. (to go)   When you _____ to school, how large were your classes?

25. (to brush)   The dog's fur has been _____ well.

26. (to like)   Don't you _____ pizza?

27. (to sit)   I _____ so long that I was stiff.

28. (to order)   A soon as the waiter comes, we shall _____.

29. (to take)   The plane _____ off on time.

30. (to try)   We are _____ to save money, but it's very difficult.

Answers begin on page 71.

Exercise 23: REVIEW OF VERBS

Directions: In each of the following exercises, four verbs have been underlined. If one of the verbs is used or formed incorrectly, blacken the space in
the answer grid under the number corresponding to it. If all of the verbs
are correct, blacken the space numbered (5).

Example: *We knew we should have went slower, but we*
               1   2

wanted to arrive before dark.
  3   4

1   2   3   4   5
‖   ▌   ‖   ‖   ‖

1. Gabe throwed the ball so hard it hit the window and
           1   2

    broke the glass, which shattered all over the ground.
    3   4

1.   1 2 3 4 5

2. No one can come if he ain't able to ride a horse and pitch
           1   2   3   4

    a tent.

2.   1 2 3 4 5

3. Federal Express should have came to pick up the package;
                     1

    if they don't come by noon, I will deliver it myself.
            2   3   4

3.   1 2 3 4 5

4. Mario has done some research on Mount St. Helens. He
          1

    has found many facts that explain how the volcano
    2   3

    formed.
    4

4.   1 2 3 4 5

5. When Prince Charles become engaged to Lady Diana
                       1

    Spencer, the newspapers ran many articles about the
                            2

    couple—how they met, where they went, etc.
                     3   4

5.   1 2 3 4 5

6. Why don't you make a new pot of coffee? Someone
        1   2

    has drunken all that was left.
    3   4

6.   1 2 3 4 5

7. We had run a mile when we noticed the fog had creeped
       1   2   3

    off the bay and begun to come inland.
                    4

7.   1 2 3 4 5

8. The Williamses will send their children to public school
                  1

    even though they wish they are able to send them to
                    2   3   4

    private school.

8.   1 2 3 4 5

9. Winter has come early this year. It's only October and
           1   2

    snow has fell twice. The cold has begun early, too.
         3   4

9.   1 2 3 4 5

(over)

10. I <u>like</u> that sportscaster! He <u>has</u> a good sense of humor,
    ₁   ₂
    and he <u>explain</u> the game well without <u>being</u> boring.

        10.   1   2   3   4   5

11. When the shirt <u>was washt</u> it <u>had</u> a white mark on it. I
    <u>scrubbed and scrubbed</u>, but the mark <u>wouldn't come</u> off.

        11.   1   2   3   4   5

12. Someone <u>rung</u> the doorbell and <u>spoiled</u> the peaceful
    evening we <u>wished</u> we <u>could have had</u> by ourselves.

        12.   1   2   3   4   5

13. The City Council <u>has voted</u> <u>to end</u> the reduced bus
    fares on Sundays. Now we <u>will have</u> <u>to paid</u> full fare for
    our shopping trips.

        13.   1   2   3   4   5

14. The egg salad <u>is spoiled</u>. It <u>wasn't</u> <u>keeped</u> in the
    refrigerator as it <u>should have been</u>.

        14.   1   2   3   4   5

15. David <u>felt</u> proud. "I <u>done</u> my best!" he <u>said</u>, and <u>took</u>
    his place in the winner's circle.

        15.   1   2   3   4   5

16. When I <u>mixed</u> the cookie dough, I <u>forgot</u> to <u>have added</u>
    the sugar and the whole batch <u>was wasted</u>.

        16.   1   2   3   4   5

17. Itzhak Perlman <u>has become</u> a famous modern violinist.
    Although he <u>had</u> polio, which <u>left</u> him unable <u>to walk</u>
    without braces, he performs all around the world.

        17.   1   2   3   4   5

18. We <u>have got</u> very health conscious; people <u>are</u> careful
    about what they <u>eat</u>, and they <u>enjoy</u> many different types
    of exercise.

        18.   1   2   3   4   5

19. Has anyone <u>relieved</u> the doorman since he <u>begun</u> his shift?
    He <u>looks</u> as if he might be <u>falling</u> asleep.

        19.   1   2   3   4   5

20. You <u>haven't</u> <u>done</u> nothing <u>to help</u> since you <u>moved</u> in
    with me!

        20.   1   2   3   4   5

Answers begin on page 71.

Exercise 24: MAKING SUBJECTS AND VERBS AGREE I

A singular subject must have a singular verb; a plural subject takes a plural verb. This is called **subject and verb agreement:**
  The winds *cause* the temperature to drop.

Text pages 92-95.
Text pages 97-98.

Directions: In each sentence below, underline the correct verb form given in parentheses.

Example: *The tomatoes (is, are) not ripe yet.*

1. Many trees (shade, shades) the park.
2. Those pencils (need, needs) sharpening.
3. Lunch (is, are) on the table.
4. They (like, likes) science fiction stories.
5. She (drink, drinks) eight glasses of water a day.
6. Your shoes (is, are) full of mud.
7. The employees (buy, buys) gifts for the boss's birthday.
8. The chairs (was, were) arranged in rows.
9. We (has, have) bologna and cheese sandwiches.
10. Problems (is, are) always coming up.
11. You (has, have) real musical talent.
12. The bees (swarm, swarms) around the flowers.
13. Marcy (curl, curls) her own hair.
14. Beauticians (charge, charges) ten dollars to set your hair.
15. Two highways (meet, meets) near the college.
16. Some guests (overstay, overstays) their welcome.
17. You (is, are) our last hope!
18. We (was, were) late for the movie.
19. They (take, takes) the train to work.
20. Drunk drivers (cause, causes) thousands of accidents each year.

Answers begin on page 72.

Exercise 25:   MAKING SUBJECTS AND VERBS AGREE II

In some sentences it will be harder to choose the correct verb form. Follow the rules below.

1) Use *don't* only for plural subjects and *doesn't* for singular subjects.
2) In sentences containing *as well as* and *together with*, the subject is not part of either of these phrases. The verb must agree with the subject.
3) The object of a preposition is never the subject of a sentence.

Text pages 102–103.

Directions: In each sentence below, underline the correct verb given in parentheses.

Example: *Green vegetables, as well as fruit, (provide, provides) vitamin C.*

1. The program (don't, doesn't) come on until 6:00 p.m.

2. Walking, as well as other exercises, (is, are) good for the heart.

3. A long skirt, together with heavy boots, (make, makes) your legs look fat.

4. The film about the trained monkeys (was, were) interesting.

5. The seats in the first row of the theater (is, are) empty.

6. The pork chops, as well as the salad, (is, are) delicious.

7. The paints in the carton on the porch (is, are) for the janitor.

8. New tires, together with a tune-up, (cost, costs) more than I can afford.

9. The books on the second shelf of the bookcase (was, were) my favorites.

10. Basement apartments in our city (don't, doesn't) rent for less than $300 a month.

11. The bills from his accident on the job (was, were) paid by the Workmen's Compensation program.

12. The glasses on the table, as well as the ones on the sink (has, have) been washed.

13. The gas stations on the corner (don't, doesn't) charge too much.

14. We (don't, doesn't) ever take a vacation.

15. George (don't, doesn't) like to go to the dentist.

Answers begin on page 72.

Exercise 26:   MAKING SUBJECTS AND VERBS AGREE III

Follow the rules given below.

1) You must decide whether *who, which,* or *that* replaces a singular or plural subject.
2) In sentences in which the verb comes before the subject (inverted word order) you must be sure to find the subject and decide if it is singular or plural.
3) In sentences that begin with *here* or *there,* you must look for the true subject of the sentence to determine the form of the verb.

Text pages 98-102.
Text pages 104-107.

Directions: In each sentence below, underline the correct verb given in parentheses.

Example: *This is one of those pens that (leak, leaks) all over.*

1. Here (is, are) the best single answer to all your questions.
2. Maxine is one of those people who (rub, rubs) me the wrong way.
3. In the Nicolet Forest (grow, grows) many kinds of fir trees.
4. There (was, were) hundreds of unhappy ticketholders who (was, were) turned away from the concert.
5. Among his records, Jack (has, have) all of the Marvin Gaye albums.
6. There (wasn't, weren't) a soul out on the street.
7. The laws which are passed by Congress (need, needs) the president's approval.
8. Down the hall (live, lives) the oldest women in the city.
9. There (go, goes) another twenty-dollar bill!
10. The groceries that I buy each week (fill, fills) two bags.
11. Sue is one of those housekeepers who (leave, leaves) everything until the last minute.
12. Firefighters are one type of worker who (put, puts) public safety before personal safety.
13. On the floor (was, were) dozens of ants.
14. From the mountains (comes, come) the cold weather.
15. Here (come, comes) the new tenants.

Answers begin on page 72.

Exercise 27: MAKING SUBJECTS AND VERBS AGREE IV: COLLECTIVE NOUNS

Learn the rules and study the examples below for making verbs agree with problem subjects.

1) Use a singular verb when the subject is a collective noun which is thought of as a single unit:
   The *crowd is* breaking up now.
   If the collective noun is meant to refer to each of the group's members, a plural verb may be needed:
   The *staff have* to get flu shots.
2) Some nouns are always plural in form. When they are singular in meaning, they require a singular verb:
   Mathematics is always hard for me.
3) Amounts and measurements used as subjects usually require singular verbs:
   Eight hours is too long to drive.

Text pages 62-63, 66.
Text pages 109-111.

Directions: In each sentence below, underline the correct verb given in parentheses.

Example: *Three weeks (is, are) a generous vacation.*

1. The news (was, were) depressing after the earthquakes.
2. Two inches (was, were) cut off Syril's hair.
3. Physics (was, were) too hard for most students.
4. The family (like, likes) to eat all of their meals together.
5. Civics (has, have) always interested me.
6. The orchestra (is, are) performing at Lincoln Center.
7. Five dollars (has, have) to last me until next Friday.
8. Economics (wasn't, weren't) taught when I was a student.
9. (Is, Are) the basketball team well-trained?
10. The team members (come, comes) in their own cars.
11. Your eyeglasses (look, looks) dirty.
12. The teens (are, is) often a time of rebellion.
13. Push-ups (develop, develops) strong arm muscles.
14. Measles (cause, causes) a red, itching rash.
15. Nine months (seem, seems) so long to be pregnant!

Answers begin on page 72.

Exercise 28:   MAKING SUBJECTS AND VERBS AGREE V: INDEFINITE PRONOUNS

Some subjects always take a singular verb even though the meaning may seem plural:

Each is in charge of his own suitcase.

The indefinite pronouns listed below always take singular verbs.

each	one	someone	somebody
either	no one	anyone	anybody
neither	everyone	nobody	everybody

Some subjects take either a singular or plural verb depending on the meaning they get from another word in the sentence:

Some of the *eggs are* cracked.

Some of the *milk is* for breakfast.

All, part, some, none, half (and other fractions) and *most* are indefinite pronouns that can take either a singular or plural verb.

Text pages 102-104.
Text pages 107-109.

Directions: In each sentence below, underline the correct verb form given in parentheses.

Example: *Everyone (want, wants) dessert.*

1. Part of the problem (is, are) our lack of free time.
2. Everyone (use, uses) her own paintbrushes.
3. Half of the boys (come, comes) from Texas.
4. Neither of the drugs (help, helps) a sore back.
5. All of the authors (sign, signs) their books at the sale.
6. Most of the clothing at the flea market (look, looks) torn and dirty.
7. Half of the payment (is, are) due this month.
8. Fifty percent of your taxes (go, goes) to the military.
9. If anybody (call, calls), I can't talk now.
10. Neither of the cabins (has, have) been rented.
11. All of that exercise (wear, wears) me out!
12. One of the movies in town (is, are) worth seeing.
13. Half of the winners (receive, receives) free dinners.
14. Each of the weekends in May (get, gets) so busy.
15. Neither of the raccoons (come, comes) near the garbage.

Answers begin on page 72.

Exercise 29:   MAKING SUBJECTS AND VERBS AGREE VI: COMPOUND SUBJECTS

A compound subject joined by *and* almost always takes a plural verb:
Cookies and donuts are very fattening.

A compound subject joined by *or, nor, neither . . . nor, either . . . or,* or *not only . . . but also* takes either a singular or plural verb depending on the part of the subject nearest to the verb:
Neither the typewriter nor the file *cabinets were* moved.
Either some squirrels or a *dog keeps* spilling our garbage.

Be careful with sentences that have a predicate nominative. The verb always agrees with the subject, not the predicate nominative:
Ham and eggs are a popular breakfast.
A popular *breakfast is* ham and eggs.

Text pages 96-98.
Text pages 100-101.

Directions: In each sentence below, underline the correct verb form given in parentheses.

Example: *Neither Bess nor her sisters (plays, play) piano.*

1. Pansies and geraniums (grow, grows) well in window boxes.

2. Woolen underwear and heavy jackets (keep, keeps) the forest rangers warm.

3. Either some earthquakes or a volcano (shake, shakes) this area from time to time.

4. Either the television or the radio (is, are) on.

5. Parents and their children (is, are) invited.

6. A doctor or a paramedic (is, are) licensed to give oxygen.

7. The animals or their keeper (leave, leaves) the gates open.

8. Horses and a sleigh (is, are) the only way to get around on this ice.

9. The lights or the iron (use, uses) enough electricity to blow a fuse.

10. Both the problems and the solution (is, are) printed in the workbook.

11. Fried chicken and spaghetti (is, are) his favorite foods.

12. Neither Joe nor his partners (know, knows) how to fix the engine.

13. A breeze and some clouds (is, are) spoiling our picnic.

14. Either the windows or the door (has, have) been left open.

15. Not only potatoes, but also dessert, (is, are) allowed on the diet.

Answers begin on page 72.

Exercise 30:   REVIEW OF SUBJECT-VERB AGREEMENT

Directions: In each sentence below, underline the correct verb form given in parentheses.

Example: *The windows and the floor (<u>need</u>, needs) washing.*

1. The curtains (don't, doesn't) close completely.
2. Everybody in the cast (has, have) rehearsal tonight.
3. The cabin in the woods (was, were) a perfect spot for our vacation.
4. He (don't, doesn't) understand English well.
5. Pretzels, as well as an apple, (was, were) our snack.
6. The problem of rats and roaches in abandoned buildings (is, are) hard to solve.
7. Gail (is, are) one of those people who cause grief wherever she goes.
8. One of those programs (was, were) supposed to be shown on television last night.
9. On the picnic table (was, were) sandwiches, potato chips, and soda pop.
10. Major Burns, as well as his captains, (inspect, inspects) the troops every day.
11. The jury (hasn't, haven't) reached a verdict.
12. Someone around here (don't, doesn't) use deodorant!
13. The family (eat, eats) meals separately.
14. Data on crime in the cities (make, makes) me afraid to go out at night.
15. The scissors (need, needs) sharpening.
16. Each nurse (has, have) his or her own station.
17. A group of vacationers (come, comes) to the beach by bus every weekend.
18. Here (grow, grows) the freshest vegetables in town.
19. Three miles (is, are) the distance to the factory.
20. Smokey and his guitar players (sound, sounds) great on the record.
21. Lemon juice, as well as artificial flavoring, (give, gives) the drinks a refreshing taste.

(over)

22. Not only string beans but also corn (add, adds) vitamins to your diet.

23. None of those items (sell, sells) rapidly.

24. The ice cream, together with all of the toppings, (look, looks) delicious.

25. Half of the cars on the road today (is, are) economy-sized models.

26. The neighbors on our block (is, are) friendly.

27. She (don't, doesn't) believe your excuse.

28. (Wasn't, Weren't) there more tickets sold than the theater could hold?

29. Paints, together with colored paper, (entertain, entertains) most children.

30. Here (come, comes) the hardest problems on the test.

Answers begin on page 72.

Exercise 31: DEFINING PRONOUNS

A **pronoun** is a word that can replace any noun and can be used in the same way as the noun it replaces:

When the pilots completed their basic training, *they* had a party.

In using pronouns, remember to do these two things:
  1) Choose correctly either subjective, objective, or possessive forms.
  2) Choose the right number and person to match the noun being replaced.

Text page 50.
Text pages 47–53.

Directions: Underline the correct pronoun form given in parentheses.

Example: *The finest mathematician is (she, her).*

1. Calvin sent (we, us) a secret message.
2. (Our, Ours) flashlight needs new batteries.
3. We need (you, your) signature.
4. The worst players were (they, them).
5. There is a telephone call for (she, her).
6. Michael painted the kitchen (hisself, himself).
7. Give (you, yourself) a pat on the back!
8. Darkness frightens (I, me).
9. (I, Me) found some plums in the refrigerator.
10. Do (you, yourself) know the way to the auditorium?
11. Janet and Sally drove home (herselves, themselves).
12. The Kleins' apartment is smaller than (ours, our's).
13. The neighbors, (she, her) and her son, came for coffee.
14. (We, Us) are going fishing.
15. Jeff loaned his fishing pole to (us, ourselves).
16. Jackie gave (he, him) a kiss.
17. The boys pay for the insurance (theirselves, themselves).
18. The prizes were (theirs, their's).
19. Minnie wants your address for (her, herself's) records.
20. The fastest swimmer was (he, him).

Answers begin on page 72.

Exercise 32: CHOOSING THE RIGHT KIND OF PRONOUN I

1) In sentences with one or more nouns and/or pronouns read the sentence without the extra nouns or pronouns to decide upon the correct forms:

> Their parents and (*they,* them) get along well.
>> (Their parents get along well. They get along well.)
>
> (*She,* Her) and (*I,* me) have the same perfume.
>> (She has the same perfume. I have the same perfume.)

2) Remember that *who* and *whoever* are used only as subjects, *whom* and *whomever* are used as anything except subjects:

> Our leader, *whom* we admire, is a genius.

Text pages 50-55. Text pages 48, 55-57.

Directions: Underline the correct pronoun form of the two given.

Example: *(Whoever, <u>Whomever</u>) you select will be your partner.*

1. Do you know (who, whom) left the message?
2. Carla and Mike and (I, me) work well together.
3. (Who, Whom) have you chosen?
4. Ask (whoever, whomever) calls to come over right away.
5. Dr. Silver saves one appointment for patients, (who, whom) have an emergency.
6. A flight attendant (who, whom) is married is separated from his or her spouse often.
7. The conductor (who, whom) we saw is James Levine (who, whom) also conducts the Metropolitan Opera Orchestra.
8. (We, Us) and (they, them) are distant relatives.
9. The loggers and (they, them) sleep in the bunk house.
10. Firemen rescued (whoever, whomever) they could.
11. (He, Him) and his motorcycle make me nervous.
12. (Who, Whom) do you wish to see?
13. Let's visit (whoever, whomever) just moved upstairs.
14. The children dislike anyone (who, whom) tells them "no."
15. (Who, Whom) in his right mind would stay awake until 4:00 a.m. every night?

Answers begin on page 73.

Exercise 33: CHOOSING THE RIGHT KIND OF PRONOUN II

Follow these three rules to help you choose the right kind of pronoun:

1) After any form of the verb *to be,* use the subjective form of the pronoun:
   It is *she.*
2) After the preposition *between,* use the objective form of the pronoun:
   The choice was between *him* and *me.*
3) After the words *than* or *as,* supply the missing part of the sentence to determine whether to use the subjective or objective form of the pronoun:
   Eric is definitely smarter than *he* (is).
   The officers know my brother better than *me.*
   (better than they know me)

Text pages 49, 52–53, 57.

Directions: Underline the correct pronoun form of the two given.

Example: *Toni Morrison is as good a writer as (her, <u>she</u>).*

1. Do you think Brooke Shields is prettier than (I, me)?
2. The first caller was (she, her).
3. Some parents let their children come between (they, them).
4. Red looks better on Wendy than (I, me).
5. Dad spends more time with Amy than with (I, me).
6. The goalie weighs twenty pounds less than (he, him).
7. In the fight between Ali and (he, him), Ali looked sharp.
8. Some countries are not as advanced as (we, us) in the area of fighting cancer.
9. No one noticed the tension between Charles and (he, him).
10. Linda Ronstadt sings that better than (she, her).
11. Their family has more money than (we, us).
12. The ambulance was going twice as fast as (we, us).
13. The best dancers are (he, him) and (she, her).
14. Our best runner has always been (he, him).
15. If you were (she, her), would you attempt the dive?
16. The best driver was (he, him).
17. Sharon has more patience than (I, me).
18. Richard Pryor tells jokes better than (he, him).
19. Between you and (I, me), I am pretty disgusted right now.
20. Mama is a better cook than (I, me).

Answers begin on page 73.

Exercise 34: CHOOSING THE RIGHT KIND OF PRONOUN III

1) When *we* or *us* is followed by a noun, mentally leave out the noun to see if the pronoun is used as a subject or object:

   We New Yorkers move fast. (We . . . move fast.)

   The children called *us* foreigners bad names. (The children called us . . . bad names.)

2) Pronouns that end in *self* or *selves* can only be used when the subject's "self" receives the action:

   He was proud of *himself.*

3) Use the possessive form of a pronoun before a gerund:

   His snoring kept everyone awake.

4) When pronouns are connected with one or more nouns, the pronoun goes last:

   Natalie and *I* took the train to work.

Text pages 51, 53-54, 57-58.

Directions: Underline the correct pronoun form of the two given.

Example: *I am tired of (you, <u>your</u>) complaining.*

1. (Your, You) cracking your gum is a bad habit.

2. An actress and (myself, I) rehearsed the lines.

3. The boss won't tolerate (me, my) smoking on the job.

4. (We, Us) senior citizens don't get a fair deal.

5. The government should send (we, us) taxpayers a refund.

6. Will (me, my) singing disturb you?

7. Glenda and (I, myself) don't get along too well.

8. City people think (we, us) small town folk are dumb.

9. No one likes (you, your) smoking in the car.

10. (You, Your) wearing an apron looks silly.

11. (We, Us) voters have a lot of power.

12. Call (we, us) servicemen whenever there's trouble.

13. Florence and (yourself, you) are late.

14. (We, Us) German-Americans are misunderstood.

15. Don't blame (we, us) men for all of women's problems.

16. Dana and (he, himself) plan to be married.

17. (You, Your) hammering has given (me, myself) a headache.

18. (We, Us) workers demand stricter safety regulations.

19. (We, Us) adults returning to school need special help.

20. This is for (you, yourself).

Answers begin on page 73.

Exercise 35:   CHOOSING THE RIGHT NUMBER AND PERSON FOR PRONOUNS I

1) When the pronoun replaces two or more nouns joined by *and*, use the plural form of the pronoun:
   Ponch and *Jon* rode *their* motorcycles through town.

2) When the pronoun replaces two nouns joined together by *or, nor, either . . . or, neither . . . nor*, or *not only . . . but also*, the pronoun agrees with the last noun in the series:
   Neither tea nor cola *drinks* list *their* caffeine content.
   Not only the dogs but also the *cat* came to *its* owner's rescue.

3) When the pronoun replaces a collective noun, use a singular pronoun when the noun is thought of as a single unit. Use a plural pronoun when the noun is thought of as separate things:
   Styx is my favorite group; *its* songs are great.
   The *staff* are doing *their* paperwork now.

Text pages 59-61.

Directions: Underline the correct pronoun of the two given.

Example: *Not only the fenders but also the chrome trim has lost (its, their) shine.*

1. Barbara and her children lost (her, their) lease.

2. Not only the residents but also the owner asked for (his, their) apartment to be painted.

3. The group holds (its, their) meetings at noon.

4. Not only hot soup but also fresh bread sent (its, their) aroma down the stairs.

5. The family are taking (its, their) showers now.

6. The movies and television have lost (its, their) appeal because of the violence in them.

7. The crowd showed (its, their) approval by clapping.

8. The circus clowns and the ringmaster took (their, his) bows.

9. The table or the chairs need (their, its) positions changed.

10. Either the fudge or the chocolate brownies left (its, their) mark on my waistline!

11. The orchestra tune up (its, their) instruments before each performance.

12. Rocks and broken glass cause (its, their) problems on the highways.

Answers begin on page 73.

Exercise 36: CHOOSING THE RIGHT NUMBER AND PERSON FOR PRONOUNS II

1) Use the singular form of the pronoun with these words:

person	neither	someone	somebody
each	no one	anyone	anybody
either	everyone	nobody	everybody

Everyone must control *his* own temper.

2) Use the pronoun *which* only for animals and things; use the pronouns *who* and *whom* only for people; use the pronoun *that* for either people or animals and things:

The dog *that* hurt its paw will be okay.
A person *who* overeats will gain weight.

Text pages 102-104, and 109-205.
Text pages 61, 63.

Directions: Underline the correct pronoun of the two given.

Example: *Anyone who forgets (his, their) keys is in trouble.*

1. The man (which, that) lives upstairs is a heavy smoker.

2. Nobody should abuse (his, their) body that way.

3. The animals (who, which) live in the sewers carry many diseases.

4. The person (who, which) called didn't leave (her, its) phone number.

5. Everybody needs a special friend of (his, their) own.

6. The birds (who, which) fly south will return in spring.

7. The women (whom, that) bowl on Wednesdays won the tournament.

8. The ad was for a person who has (his, their) own car.

9. The people (whom, which) we like best are the quietest.

10. I see the dog (who, which) bit me!

11. Nobody can cope with (her, their) problems better than my sister.

12. People (whose, that) drink shouldn't drive.

13. If neither wants (his, their) dessert, I'll eat both.

14. The trees (who, which) stand near the gate are losing their leaves.

15. Our fish, (who, which) are named Frick and Frack, are blue paradise fish.

Answers begin on page 73.

Exercise 37:   PRONOUN REVIEW

Directions: If there is an error in a sentence, blacken the space in the answer grid under the number corresponding to it. If there is no error, blacken the space numbered (5).

Example: *President Kennedy said <u>we</u> citizens should help*
                              1
<u>our</u> country by aiding in <u>its</u> development and by
   2   3
improving <u>our</u> own physical fitness.
            4

     1   2   3   4   5

1. <u>Us</u> Californians don't like <u>your</u> calling <u>us</u> crazy the way
   1   2   3
   <u>you</u> do.
   4

     1.   1   2   3   4   5

2. Some people <u>who</u> have problems need help from another
              1
   person <u>whom</u> can listen to <u>them</u> and offer <u>his</u> advice.
          2   3   4

     2.   1   2   3   4   5

3. Can <u>you</u> do this <u>yourself</u>, or should <u>I</u> call someone <u>which</u>
       1   2   3   4
   can help?

     3.   1   2   3   4   5

4. Everyone left <u>their</u> boots on the doorstep; <u>no one</u> will be
                1   2
   able to find <u>his</u> own later. I'm glad <u>mine</u> are labeled.
                3   4

     4.   1   2   3   4   5

5. Call for <u>me</u> when <u>you</u> need a hand with those tires of
            1   2
   <u>your's</u> and <u>I'll</u> come right over.
     3   4

     5.   1   2   3   4   5

6. Neither Matilda nor <u>her</u> brothers brought <u>their</u> skis. <u>They</u>
                      1   2   3
   expect to use <u>ours</u>.
                 4

     6.   1   2   3   4   5

7. It was <u>me</u> <u>who</u> called to <u>you</u> from <u>my</u> window.
          1   2   3   4

     7.   1   2   3   4   5

8. Fill <u>everyone's</u> glass so <u>they</u> can toast the winners, <u>he</u> and
        1   2   3
   <u>she</u>.
   4

     8.   1   2   3   4   5

9. <u>Them</u> are the ones <u>that</u> <u>we</u> elected to <u>our</u> Congress.
   1   2   3   4

     9.   1   2   3   4   5

10. The photographer put <u>its</u> camera in <u>its</u> bag after taking
                         1   2
    pictures of <u>us</u> performers in <u>our</u> costumes.
               3   4

     10.   1   2   3   4   5

11. It upsets <u>me</u> when <u>someone</u> like <u>yourself</u> doesn't do <u>his</u>
              1   2   3   4
    share of work.

     11.   1   2   3   4   5

(over)

12. Not only I, but also my sons, have their suitcases, which are in the car.
    1   2   3   4

    12. 1 2 3 4 5

13. We teachers don't care whom helps you, as long as your answers are correct.
    1   2   3   4

    13. 1 2 3 4 5

14. The sheriff himself and him ordered us riders off their property.
    1   2   3   4

    14. 1 2 3 4 5

15. The directions which you gave me got myself all mixed up.
    1   2   3   4

    15. 1 2 3 4 5

16. The girls and I met the person that we had heard about from you.
    1   2   3   4

    16. 1 2 3 4 5

17. We parents resent you interfering with how we raise our children.
    1   2   3   4

    17. 1 2 3 4 5

18. Dr. Skin says us runners may have our problems with our feet when we age.
    1   2   3   4

    18. 1 2 3 4 5

19. This is the medicine for yourself; you must take it for your high blood pressure.
    1   2   3   4

    19. 1 2 3 4 5

20. The bee that stung me was bigger than any that I had ever seen.
    1   2   3   4

    20. 1 2 3 4 5

21. The sewers which backed up into our basements caused us homeowners to complain to whoever was nearby.
    1   2   3   4

    21. 1 2 3 4 5

22. Someone whom loves his children will usually raise them correctly.
    1   2   3   4

    22. 1 2 3 4 5

23. If anybody loses their ticket, report it to someone wearing an usher's uniform.
    1   2   3   4

    23. 1 2 3 4 5

24. These pens run out of their ink quickly; the problem with them is that you can't see how much ink is left in it.
    1   2   3   4

    24. 1 2 3 4 5

25. Us city dwellers have our needs for privacy, but we must learn to satisfy these needs in an environment which is crowded.
    1   2   3   4

    25. 1 2 3 4 5

Answers begin on page 73.

Exercise 38: ADJECTIVES AND ADVERBS

An **adjective** is a word that describes a noun to tell what kind, which one, or how many:

The *tiny* baby is struggling for life.

An **adverb** is a word that modifies a verb, an adverb, or an adjective to tell how, when, where, or to what extent:

I began a new job *yesterday*.

Text pages 119–121.

Directions: On the first blank at the right of each sentence, tell whether the word underlined in the sentence is an adjective or an adverb. On the second blank, tell what word in the sentence is modified by the adjective or adverb.

Example: *A tall man called for you.*

adjective
man

1. Your suit is very stylish.

1. _____

2. Some flowers seem to attract bees more than others.

2. _____

3. The orange blanket belongs in the back bedroom.

3. _____

4. Jim Fixx eats that crunchy cereal I see advertised on TV.

4. _____

5. The chairs noisily scraped on the floor when we stood up.

5. _____

6. Salted peanuts cost $.50 a bag.

6. _____

7. The detective crept cautiously out of his hiding place.

7. _____

8. Come here and let me see you.

8. _____

9. Let's go to the laundromat now.

9. _____

10. There are several movies that are worth seeing.

10. _____

11. We finished the bread today.

11. _____

12. Lukewarm water is best for most washing.

12. _____

13. An overweight person broke the fragile antique chair.

13. _____

14. Jan was truly sorry to be late for the wedding.

14. _____

15. The hijacking victims were extremely frightened, but not hurt.

15. _____

Answers begin on page 73.

Exercise 39: THE FORM OF ADJECTIVES AND ADVERBS

The rules below will help distinguish between adjectives and adverbs.
1) Most adverbs are formed by adding *ly* to the adjective:
   quiet, quietly
2) Adjectives that end in *le* are made into adverbs by changing the ending to *ly:*
   probable, probably
3) Adjectives that end in *l* are made into adverbs by adding *ly:*
   careful, carefully
4) Adjectives that end in *ll* are made into adverbs by adding *y:*
   dull, dully
5) Adjectives that end in *ic* are usually made into adverbs by adding *ally:*
   historic, historically
6) Some adjectives already end in *ly* and remain the same when used as an adverb:
   daily; early
7) Some adjectives that do not end in *ly* remain the same when used as an adverb:
   fast; late; hard
8) Some adjectives change spelling when they are made into adverbs:
   easy, easily; true, truly
9) Some adjectives can never be used as adverbs:
   lonely; friendly

Text pages 121-123.

Directions: Underline the correct adjective or adverb form of the two given in parentheses.

Example: *The dance concert progressed (smooth, <u>smoothly</u>.)*

1. We ate (hearty, heartily) at the buffet.
2. Squeeze the tomatoes (gentle, gently).
3. Jed gave a (tearful, tearfully) farewell.
4. The water heater works (poor, poorly).
5. Natalie Cole sings (romantic, romantically) songs.
6. Run (quick, quickly) and spread the alarm.
7. Is that a (real, really) Indian arrowhead?
8. (Squeaky, Squeakily), the door opened.
9. I fell (weary, wearily) into bed.
10. A (loud, loudly) crash woke me up.
11. The (quiet, quietly) ticking of the clock won't disturb you.
12. It is a (basic, basically) rule that you replace all lost parts.
13. Try (hard, hardly) to be on time.
14. Judi arrived so (late, lately) we left without her.

Answers begin on page 73.

Exercise 40: USING ADJECTIVES AND ADVERBS CORRECTLY I: PREDICATE ADJECTIVES

Use an adjective after forms of the verb *to be* and other linking verbs. An adjective in this position is called a **predicate adjective**:
  She looks *good*.
  The child has been *bad* all week.

Never use *well* or *badly* as predicate adjectives. They are adverbs.

Note: There is one exception to this rule. When speaking about health, *well* is used:
  The patient feels *well* today.

Text pages 124–125, 131.

Directions: Underline the correct form of the two given in parentheses.

Example: *Gina felt (<u>bad</u>, badly) about her mistake.*

1. The day looks (good, well) for our picnic.

2. The rotten eggs smell (awful, awfully).

3. I cut myself (bad, badly) on the sharp edge of the can.

4. I feel so (sore, sorely) I can't move.

5. Rachel sews (good, well).

6. The children became (noisy, noisily) on the long bus ride.

7. They behaved (good, well) at the museum, however.

8. The book is (easy, easily) for most students.

9. Sharona looked (beautiful, beautifully) in her bathing suit.

10. Pedro looked (good, well) in his suit, too.

11. His arms felt (strong, strongly) as he carried me to safety.

12. She always grows (nervous, nervously) on Sunday night.

13. The doctor says I will be (good, well) by tomorrow.

14. Your cooking always smells so (good, well).

15. Our cat can't smell (good, well) enough to catch a mouse.

16. Your shirt looks (dirty, dirtily).

17. That girl appears (familiar, familiarly) to me.

18. When will you be (ready, readily)?

19. Do you feel (well, good) enough to travel?

20. The days become noticeably (short, shortly) in the fall.

(over)

21. Jared feels (eager, eagerly) about his new hobby.

22. I'm pleased that you're feeling (well, good) so soon after your operation.

23. How (dull, dully) the windows look.

24. I have never been so (proud, proudly) of my wife as I am today.

25. A wool-lined coat will keep you quite (warm, warmly) during the cold winter months.

26. After eating this piece of watermelon, everything else tastes (sour, sourly).

27. That candidate has an advantage in the election; she looks so (good, well) on television.

28. No one felt as (sick, sickly) as Pete when he got the layoff notice.

29. Despite his lengthy vacation, he still looked (bad, badly) when I saw him.

30. Almost any news sounds (well, good) when you're far away from home.

Answers begin on page 74.

Exercise 41:   USING ADJECTIVES AND ADVERBS CORRECTLY II

1. When you use such negative adverbs as *not, hardly,* and *scarcely,* don't use any other negatives in the sentence.

2. Use the adjective *this* for singular nouns that are close by. Use the adjective *that* for singular nouns that are some distance away:

    I prefer *this* seat by the door.

    Can you see *that* car in the lot?

    Use *these* for plural nouns that are close by.

    Use *those* for plural nouns that are some distance away.

    These shoes kill my feet.

    Those railroad tracks need repairing.

    Only use *this* to refer to a specific person or thing.

    Never say *this here* or *that there.*

    Never use the objective pronoun *them* to point to something.

3. Use *an* before nouns that begin with a vowel sound. For all other words, use *a:*

    an eagle; *a* historic event; *an* hour

    For words that begin with the vowels *u* or *eu* pronounced like *you,* use *a:*

    a usual event; *a* eulogy

Text pages 132-133.

Directions: If one of the four words underlined in each sentence below is incorrectly used, blacken the space in the answer grid under the number corresponding to it. If all the words are used correctly, blacken the space numbered (5).

Example: <u>An</u> <u>elderly</u> gentleman has reserved <u>this here</u> study
       1   2   3
booth for <u>an</u> hour.

    1 2 **3** 4 5

1. I <u>only</u> have a <u>few</u> dollars to spare <u>now</u>, but <u>tomorrow</u> I'll be rich.

    1. 1 2 3 4 5

2. Sal feels <u>real</u> <u>bad</u> about his <u>silly</u> mistake <u>downstairs</u>.

    2. 1 2 3 4 5

3. Barbara has <u>always</u> been <u>an</u> <u>extremely</u> <u>difficult</u> person to live with.

    3. 1 2 3 4 5

4. The <u>head</u> waiter wants to become <u>expert</u> at managing <u>an</u> <u>European</u> cafe soon.

    4. 1 2 3 4 5

(over)

5. We were <u>sadly</u> <u>disappointed</u> to hear about your father's   **5.**   1   2   3   4   5

      ¹   ²
<u>suddenly</u> and <u>unexpected</u> death.

   ³   ⁴

6. The train <u>hardly</u> <u>never</u> starts out <u>late</u>, but it <u>often</u> arrives   **6.**   1   2   3   4   5

         ¹   ²   ³   ⁴
late.

7. The <u>golden</u> loaves of <u>warm</u> bread smelled <u>especially</u>   **7.**   1   2   3   4   5

     ¹   ²   ³
<u>freshly</u>.

⁴

8. <u>Those</u> stockings I am wearing <u>now</u> are <u>too</u> <u>baggy</u>.   **8.**   1   2   3   4   5

  ¹   ²   ³ ⁴

9. An <u>honorable</u> man would return <u>this</u> <u>here</u> <u>lost</u> money.   **9.**   1   2   3   4   5

    ¹   ²   ³   ⁴

10. The <u>dainty</u> ballerina danced <u>graceful</u> across the stage. She   **10.**   1   2   3   4   5

     ¹   ²
seemed <u>so</u> <u>perfect</u> as to be unreal.

        ³   ⁴

11. Cecilia is <u>an</u> alto in the church choir; she sings <u>beautifully</u>   **11.**   1   2   3   4   5

         ¹   ²
and <u>always</u> has <u>a</u> important part.

     ³   ⁴

12. Do you like <u>these</u> <u>here</u> hats, or do you like <u>those</u>   **12.**   1   2   3   4   5

            ¹   ²   ³
over there with <u>those</u> tassels?

               ⁴

13. <u>An</u> umbrella is <u>always</u> <u>an</u> <u>wise</u> investment in the spring.   **13.**   1   2   3   4   5

 ¹   ²   ³ ⁴

14. I <u>can</u> <u>hardly</u> believe the prices of <u>these</u> cars; <u>those</u> we   **14.**   1   2   3   4   5

  ¹   ²   ³   ⁴
saw last week were much cheaper.

15. John found <u>an</u> <u>unbelievable</u> amount of money hidden in   **15.**   1   2   3   4   5

         ¹   ²
<u>this</u> mattress. He says fate gave him <u>this</u> good fortune.

³   ⁴

Answers begin on page 74.

Exercise 42: USING ADJECTIVES AND ADVERBS FOR COMPARISON I

Whenever you use an adverb or an adjective to compare two or more nouns or pronouns, use the form that is correct for the number of things being compared.

1) To show that two nouns are equal:
   Genevieve is *as clever as* Marge.
   Leatrice swims *as easily as* Carl.
2) To show that two nouns are unequal:
   Today is *warmer* than yesterday.
   You walk *more quickly* than Florence.
3) To show that three or more nouns are unequal:
   Genevieve is the *cleverest* person I know.
   Bones is the *least playful* dog I've ever seen.

Text pages 126-128.

Directions: Use the correct form of the adjective or adverb before each sentence below to fill in the blank correctly.

Example: *(busy) We have been* ___*busier*___ *than we expected this summer.*

1. (small) Which was the _____ of the Seven Dwarves?

2. (hard) This course is _____ than it was supposed to be.

3. (beautiful) Leontyne Price sings _____ than any other living opera star.

4. (queer) We had the _____ experience of our lifetimes last night.

5. (patient) Midge is _____ than I. That's why she is able to wait so long for him.

6. (deep) Lake Thompson is the _____ of all the lakes around Rhinelander.

7. (loud) The one who laughed last laughed _____ of all.

8. (popular) John Kennedy was one of the _____ presidents our country has ever had.

9. (eager) Doug is _____ than Joe is to get his high school diploma.

10. (rainy) This is the _____ April we have ever had.

(over)

11.   (happy) Gabriel is one of the _____
      children I have ever met.

12.   (long) Which live _____ as pets, goldfish or
      turtles?

13.   (sloppy) Some of the _____ people in the
      office are very neat at home.

14.   (sick) I was _____ when I had the flu than
      when I had pneumonia.

15.   (silent) The engine in the new car runs _____
      than any I have ever heard.

Answers begin on page 74.

Exercise 43: USING ADJECTIVES AND ADVERBS FOR COMPARISON II

1) Use only one form of comparison, not two:
   Jan is *smarter* than her sister.
   (NOT: *more smarter*)
2) Long adjectives (three or more syllables) and adverbs that end in *ly* can never be used with an *er* or *est* ending:
   Gran is *more impatient* than ever.
   (NOT: *impatienter*)
3) Some adjectives and adverbs have irregular forms. The text lists common irregular forms.

Text pages 127-128.

Directions: Fill in the blank with the correct comparative adjective or adverb form of the word underlined in each sentence.

Example: *In Japan, Yoko is a popular girl's name, but Yasuko is <u>more popular</u>.*

1. I felt <u>bad</u> before, but I feel even _____ now.

2. You may be <u>hungry</u>, but I am definitely the _____ person in this house.

3. Due to her excellent teaching, Marva Collins's students go <u>far</u>—much _____ than students in public schools.

4. Today is <u>hot</u>, and tomorrow is predicted to be the _____ day of the year.

5. The ads say this cereal has <u>more</u> raisins than other brands, but I think the store-brand has the _____ raisins of all.

6. If you think Melvin is <u>ugly</u>, you should see his brother; he is much _____.

7. Nurses handle babies <u>gently</u>, but new mothers handle them the _____ of all.

8. Cathy wants <u>curly</u> hair; this permanent promises the _____ hair possible from a box.

9. Ann is <u>heavy</u>, but she use to be even _____.

(over)

10. I can handle math problems <u>easily</u>, but grammar is the
    _____.

11. Jerry is <u>tall</u>, but he is not the _____ boy in
    his class.

12. The snow is <u>deep</u> now, and it will be even _____
    in a few hours.

13. I have <u>fewer</u> problems than most people; my sister has
    _____ problems than I do.

14. All doctors work <u>carefully</u>, but surgeons must work the
    _____ of all doctors.

15. That record sounds <u>good</u> and this one sounds a little
    _____.

16. Many guests were <u>late</u>, but our next-door neighbors were
    the _____ of all.

17. Detroit is <u>far</u> from our town; it is _____
    than we can drive in one day.

18. You thought you were <u>poor</u>? The people upstairs are the
    _____ people I have ever known.

19. Yesterday was <u>rainy</u>, and today is _____.

20. The seam on your dress is <u>uneven</u>. Now you have made it
    worse! It is _____ than it was.

Answers begin on page 74.

Exercise 44:   ADJECTIVE AND ADVERB REVIEW

Directions: In each of the following sentences, four words have been underlined. If one of these words is incorrectly used in the sentence, blacken the
space in the answer key under the number corresponding to it. If all of the
words are used correctly, blacken the space numbered (5).

Example: *Yesterday Scott didn't look well, and today he feels*
            1   2   3
sickly.
  4

        1 2 3 4 5

1. New Orleans is <u>more close</u> to Miami than Atlanta, but I'd
                        1
    rather drive <u>farther</u> and be able to visit my <u>best</u> friends
                     2   3
    <u>there</u>.
      4

    1. 1 2 3 4 5

2. One of the <u>hardest</u> things the doctor had <u>ever</u> done was to
                    1   2
    tell the children they had <u>only</u> a <u>few</u> months to live.
                                   3   4

    2. 1 2 3 4 5

3. Mario sings <u>good</u>, Luis sings <u>even</u> <u>better</u>, and Theresa
                    1   2   3
    sings <u>best</u>.
            4

    3. 1 2 3 4 5

4. Eat <u>less</u> calories and you will <u>soon</u> weigh <u>less</u> and have
            1   2   3
    <u>more</u> energy.
       4

    4. 1 2 3 4 5

5. Dan skated <u>well</u> but took <u>too</u> <u>much</u> <u>crazy</u> chances; now he
                   1   2   3   4
    is in the hospital.

    5. 1 2 3 4 5

6. Freddi is <u>definitely</u> <u>brighter</u> than her boss, who insists that
                  1   2
    <u>all</u> employees follow instructions <u>exact</u> as she gives them.
       3   4

    6. 1 2 3 4 5

7. <u>Tonight</u> was <u>so</u> <u>darkly</u> that we couldn't see <u>farther</u> than
       1   2   3   4
    three feet.

    7. 1 2 3 4 5

8. Visit us <u>soon</u>; we'll be <u>real</u> <u>glad</u> to show you <u>around</u>.
                 1   2   3   4

    8. 1 2 3 4 5

9. We <u>have</u> <u>hardly</u> caught <u>no</u> fish for <u>an</u> hour.
          1   2   3   4

    9. 1 2 3 4 5

10. <u>There</u> is <u>this</u> town <u>somewhere</u> in Canada <u>where</u> everyone
       1   2   3   4
    uses sleds instead of cars.

    10. 1 2 3 4 5

(over)

11. If you make <u>nasty</u> statements, you will <u>soon</u> be known as
the <u>meanest</u> person <u>around</u>.

11. 1 2 3 4 5

12. I am <u>especially</u> <u>happily</u> that you appreciate <u>fine</u> cooking
and <u>leisurely</u> dining.

12. 1 2 3 4 5

13. Joe's comments are <u>awful</u> <u>insensitive</u>; you'd think he'd be
<u>more careful</u> than he <u>usually</u> is.

13. 1 2 3 4 5

14. The doorbell's <u>loud</u> ringing disturbed us just before we fell
asleep. It was <u>very</u> <u>hard</u> to become <u>sleepily</u> again.

14. 1 2 3 4 5

15. This <u>hardly</u> costs <u>no</u> money. It is <u>truly</u> a <u>good</u> deal.

15. 1 2 3 4 5

Answers begin on page 74.

Final Skills Inventory: GRAMMAR AND USAGE

Directions: In each of the following sentences, four words or groups of words have been underlined. If one of these is an error in grammar and usage, blacken the space in the answer key under the number corresponding to it. If there is no error, blacken the space numbered (5).

Example: *She's a much better vocalist than me, but I still enjoy*
             1   2

    singing with the city's choir.
          3   4

                      1   2   3   4   5

1. Shoes often conforms to the feet of the person who wears them.
    1   2   3   4
    1. 1   2   3   4   5

2. Its raining hard now, but it will probably clear by morning.
    1   2   3   4
    2. 1   2   3   4   5

3. The weatherman said he predicted a cloudy day and was surprised by the sunshine.
                1   2   3   4
    3. 1   2   3   4   5

4. This type of a weekend vacation helps more than a big trip.
    1   2   3   4
    4. 1   2   3   4   5

5. Us prisoners were afraid the warden would poison us with spoiled food.
    1   2   3   4
    5. 1   2   3   4   5

6. The fish bited the bait and was caught easily.
        1   2   3   4
    6. 1   2   3   4   5

7. The firemen came quick in response to our frantic call.
        1   2   3   4
    7. 1   2   3   4   5

8. Someone mistakenly took my coat instead of theirs.
        1   2 3   4
    8. 1   2   3   4   5

9. The announcer which read the bad news was badly shaken.
             1   2   3   4
    9. 1   2   3   4   5

10. Who told you to whom the gift was to be sent?
    1   2   3   4
    10. 1   2   3   4   5

11. Many people were hurt when the dam bursted.
    1   2   3   4
    11. 1   2   3   4   5

12. Not only is my friends loyal, but also they have good senses of humor.
    1   2   3   4
    12. 1   2   3   4   5

13. If either of the stolen watchs is found, I will be surprised.
      1   2   3 4
    13. 1   2   3   4   5

14. It cost least to repair our car than to buy a new one.
      1   2   3   4
    14. 1   2   3   4   5

15. Kate has been real relaxed since the baby stopped her crying.
        1   2   3   4
    15. 1   2   3   4   5

16. It don't pay to eat at home these days.
      1   2   3   4
    16. 1   2   3   4   5

17. All of the photos in them albums are from high school.
         1   2   3 4
    17. 1   2   3   4   5

18. Neither the driver nor his passengers wants to stop for lunch.
    1   2   3   4
    18. 1   2   3   4   5

(over)

19. When darkness <u>fell</u> we <u>had</u> <u>took</u> our tents out, but <u>had</u> not pitched
    ₁   ₂ ₃   ₄
    them yet.

    19.   1   2   3   4   5

20. <u>Bess'</u> job, <u>as well as</u> her childcare <u>duties</u>, <u>seems</u> to be too much for her.
    ₁   ₂   ₃   ₄

    20.   1   2   3   4   5

21. Do <u>you</u> ever ask <u>yourself</u> <u>whom</u> is in charge of <u>your</u> children on the
       ₁   ₂   ₃   ₄
    school bus?

    21.   1   2   3   4   5

22. Neither Marlene nor Jessica <u>plays</u> as <u>well</u> as <u>you</u> or <u>me</u>.
                                ₁   ₂   ₃   ₄

    22.   1   2   3   4   5

23. After five <u>minutes'</u> practice on the ice, <u>I</u> <u>had</u> <u>fell</u> ten times.
              ₁   ₂ ₃ ₄

    23.   1   2   3   4   5

24. <u>They</u> <u>who</u> complain earn <u>themselves</u> a <u>bad</u> reputation.
    ₁ ₂   ₃   ₄

    24.   1   2   3   4   5

25. <u>You</u> <u>drinking</u> so <u>much</u> beer is <u>surely</u> a threat to your health.
    ₁ ₂   ₃   ₄

    25.   1   2   3   4   5

26. The salad contains lettuce, <u>tomatos</u>, <u>olives</u>, <u>mushrooms</u>, and bean
                                ₁   ₂   ₃
    <u>sprouts</u>.
    ₄

    26.   1   2   3   4   5

27. <u>Pinching pennies</u> <u>is</u> a way of life in our house; <u>save</u> is always
    ₁   ₂ ₃   ₄
    encouraged.

    27.   1   2   3   4   5

28. Not one of the <u>guests</u> <u>offered</u> to <u>clean</u> up after <u>themselves</u>.
                   ₁   ₂   ₃   ₄

    28.   1   2   3   4   5

29. Everyone in the car pool <u>drives</u> <u>much</u> faster than <u>me</u> but never <u>has</u>
                            ₁   ₂   ₃   ₄
    an accident.

    29.   1   2   3   4   5

30. New types of scalpels cut <u>more</u> <u>cleanly</u> and cause <u>fewer</u> <u>bleeding</u>
                             ₁   ₂   ₃   ₄
    than metal scalpels.

    30.   1   2   3   4   5

31. <u>Jason</u> <u>running</u> around without a jacket led to <u>his</u> <u>catching</u> a bad cold.
    ₁   ₂   ₃   ₄

    31.   1   2   3   4   5

32. "<u>Whose</u> number <u>hasn't</u> been <u>call</u> yet?" asked the <u>salesperson</u>.
     ₁   ₂   ₃   ₄

    32.   1   2   3   4   5

33. <u>It's</u> remarkable how <u>quickly</u> the mother dog had <u>its</u> litter clean and
    ₁   ₂   ₃
    <u>comfortably</u> nursing.
    ₄

    33.   1   2   3   4   5

34. Of all the <u>types</u> of wine I <u>have</u> <u>drunk</u>, I like chianti <u>more</u>.
              ₁   ₂ ₃   ₄

    34.   1   2   3   4   5

35. Chuck looked <u>so</u> <u>confidently</u> we were sure <u>he</u> had <u>won</u> his case.
                ₁ ₂   ₃   ₄

    35.   1   2   3   4   5

36. The horse <u>who</u> is <u>being</u> <u>trained</u> is <u>surely</u> a champion.
             ₁   ₂ ₃   ₄

    36.   1   2   3   4   5

37. <u>Who</u> <u>sings</u> <u>best</u>, Charlotte, or <u>I</u>?
    ₁ ₂   ₃   ₄

    37.   1   2   3   4   5

38. <u>Grandma's</u> three <u>daughter-in-laws</u> and their <u>children</u> visit her on
    ₁   ₂   ₃
    <u>holidays</u>.
    ₄

    38.   1   2   3   4   5

39. The actors <u>are</u> <u>so</u> <u>professionally</u> that <u>they</u> never miss a cue.
              ₁ ₂ ₃   ₄

    39.   1   2   3   4   5

40. Of <u>all</u> the <u>people</u> on the block, the Jeffersons <u>seem</u> <u>happier</u>.
       ₁   ₂   ₃   ₄

    40.   1   2   3   4   5

41. <u>Can</u> someone <u>from</u> the main office <u>deliver</u> the package <u>themselves</u>?
     1   2   3   4

41. 1 2 3 4 5

42. <u>How</u> <u>sudden</u> the children <u>seem</u> to have become <u>young</u> adults.
    1   2   3   4

42. 1 2 3 4 5

43. If <u>you</u> don't stop <u>your</u> <u>drink</u>, you will do serious harm to <u>yourself</u>.
       1   2   3

43. 1 2 3 4 5

44. The <u>most small</u> pets I have ever seen are "Sea Monkeys," <u>which</u> are
       1   2

    <u>really</u> <u>tiny</u> shrimp.
      3   4

44. 1 2 3 4 5

45. The <u>people's</u> <u>choices</u> <u>were</u> the same as <u>our's</u>.
       1   2   3   4

45. 1 2 3 4 5

46. The <u>historic</u> event was recorded <u>immediately</u> and <u>permanent</u> for
      1   2   3

    future <u>generations</u>.
            4

46. 1 2 3 4 5

47. <u>Heroes</u> and <u>volunteers</u> received <u>their</u> <u>much-deserved</u> awards.
    1   2   3   4

47. 1 2 3 4 5

48. Joan <u>doesn't</u> look <u>nicely</u> today, but she should look <u>better</u> <u>soon</u>.
       1   2   3   4

48. 1 2 3 4 5

49. The person <u>which</u> drove the truck <u>that</u> overturned wasn't <u>even</u> <u>hurt</u>.
           1   2   3   4

49. 1 2 3 4 5

50. Howard is <u>always</u> <u>cheerfuller</u> than his wife, who <u>never</u> seems <u>happy</u>.
          1   2   3   4

50. 1 2 3 4 5

Answers and explanations begin on page 67.

FINAL SKILLS INVENTORY EVALUATION CHART

Directions: After completing the Final Skills Inventory, check your answers by using the Final Skills Inventory Answers and Explanations, pages 67–68. Write the total number of your *correct* answers for each skill area in the blank boxes below. If you have *more than one incorrect* answer in any skill area, you need more practice. Pages to study in your textbook (Contemporary's *GED Test 1: The Writing Skills Test*) are listed in the **Text Pages** column. To find out which edition of the text you have, turn to the copyright page in the front of the text. Look for the year next to "Copyright ©." Pages to study in this workbook (Contemporary's *Grammar and Usage*) are listed in the last column.

Skill Area	Item Numbers	Total	Number Correct	Text Pages (1985 editions)	Text Pages (1988, later ed.)	Workbook Pages
Plural Nouns	13, 26, 38	3	_____	34–37	45–47	18–20
Possessive Nouns	2, 25, 31, 45	4	_____	37–38	48–50	22
Countable Nouns	4, 30	2	_____	39–40	*	23
Gerunds	27, 43	2	_____	31	*	24–26
Verb Tense	6, 11, 19, 23, 32	5	_____	70–87, 91–92	71–91	30–32
Subject-Verb Agreement	1, 12, 16, 20	4	_____	97–118	92–104	35–40
Pronoun Case	5, 17, 21, 22, 29	5	_____	48–59	50–55	43–46
Pronoun Number	8, 28, 41	3	_____	60–62	201–203	47–48
Pronoun Person	9, 36, 49	3	_____	62–64	203–205	47–48
Adjective Form	35, 39, 48	3	_____	121–123	*	52
Adverb Form	7, 15, 42, 46	4	_____	121–123	*	52
Adjective Comparison	40, 44, 50	3	_____	126–130	*	57–60
Adverb Comparison	14, 34, 37	3	_____	126–130	*	57–60

Note: *A score of 33 or more correct is considered passing for this Inventory.*
These topics are not directly tested in 1988 and later versions of the GED Writing Skills Test.

Answers and Explanations: FINAL SKILLS INVENTORY

Directions: After completing the Final Skills Inventory (pages 63–65), use the Answers and Explanations to check your work. *On these pages,* circle the number of each item you correctly answered. Then turn to the Final Skills Inventory Evaluation Chart (page 66) and follow the directions given.

1. **(2)** The plural verb *conform* is needed because the simple subject *Shoes* is plural.

2. **(1)** The contraction *It's* is needed; it means *it is*. *Its* is a possessive pronoun.

3. **(5)** No error

4. **(3)** The word *a* is not needed. The correct expression is *This type of* followed by the noun *weekend*.

5. **(1)** The subjective pronoun *We* is needed.

6. **(2)** The correct past tense of the verb *bite* is *bit*.

7. **(2)** The adverb *quickly* is needed to tell *when* the firemen came.

8. **(4)** The singular pronoun *his* (or *hers*) should be used to refer to *someone*, which is singular.

9. **(1)** The pronoun *who* is needed. *Which* refers only to animals and things.

10. **(5)** No error.

11. **(4)** The correct past tense of the verb *burst* is *burst*.

12. **(2)** The plural verb *are* is needed because the subject *friends* is plural.

13. **(3)** The correct plural of *watch* is *watches*.

14. **(2)** The correct adverb for comparing two unlike verbs is *less*. *Least* can only be used to compare three or more things.

15. **(2)** The adverb form *really* is needed to tell *to what extent* Kate has been relaxed.

16. **(1)** The singular verb *doesn't* is needed because the subject, *It*, is singular.

17. **(2)** The objective pronoun *them* can never be used as an adjective. The correct word is *those*.

18. **(4)** The plural verb *want* is needed to agree with the closest subject, *passengers*, which is plural. In a *neither . . . nor* sentence, the verb should agree with the closest subject.

19. **(3)** The correct past participle form is *taken*.

20. **(1)** The correct possessive form of *Bess* is *Bess's*.

21. **(3)** The subjective form *who* is needed as the subject of the verb *is*.

22. **(4)** The subjective form *I* is needed. The sentence really means that the others don't play as well as *I* play.

23. **(4)** The correct past participle form is *fallen*.

24. **(5)** No error.

25. **(1)** The possessive form *Your* is needed before the gerund *drinking*.

26. **(1)** The correct plural of *tomato* is *tomatoes*.

27. **(4)** The gerund form *saving* is needed as the subject of the verb *is*.

28. **(4)** The singular pronoun *himself* (or *herself*) is needed because it refers to *one*, which is singular.

29. **(3)** The subjective pronoun *I* is needed to express the comparison that everyone drives faster than *I* drive.

30. **(3)** The adjective *less* is needed because *bleeding* is an uncountable noun.

31. **(1)** The possessive form *Jason's* is needed to explain whose running around led to catching a cold.

32. **(3)** The correct past participle form is *called*.

33. **(5)** No error.

34. **(4)** *Most* is needed to show a comparison of more than two things.

35. **(2)** The adjective form *confident* is needed after the linking verb *looked*.

36. **(1)** The pronoun *which* is needed. *Who* refers only to people.

37. **(3)** The adverb form *better* is needed because only two things are being compared.

38. **(2)** The correct plural is *daughters-in-law*.

39. **(3)** The adjective form *professional* is needed after the linking verb *are*.

40. **(4)** The adjective form *happiest* is needed because more than two people are being compared.

41. **(4)** The singular pronoun *himself* (or *herself*) is needed because it refers to *someone*, which is singular.

42. **(2)** The adverb form *suddenly* is needed.

43. **(3)** The gerund form *drinking* is needed as the direct object of the verb *stop*.

44. **(1)** The correct adjective form is *smallest*. It shows comparison between three or more things.

45. **(4)** The correct spelling of the possessive is *ours*. No apostrophe is used.

46. **(3)** The adverb form *permanently* is needed. It tells how the event was recorded.

47. **(5)** No error.

48. **(2)** The adjective form *nice* is needed.

49. **(1)** The pronoun *who* or *that* should be used to refer to a person.

50. **(2)** The correct comparative adjective form is *more cheerful*.

Complete the Final Skills Inventory Chart on page 66.

ANSWER KEY

Exercise 1
1. dentist works
2. weight-lifters practiced
3. prices have gone
4. operator has been
5. center opens
6. mother is moving
7. partner will deliver
8. creams prevent
9. David left
10. chef prepared
11. article moved
12. judge declared
13. juice is
14. runners were
15. reviewers say

Exercise 2
1. S
2. F
3. F
4. F
5. S
6. S
7. F
8. F
9. S
10. F
11. F
12. S
13. F
14. S
15. F
16. F
17. S
18. F
19. S
20. F

Exercise 3
1. storm was
2. (you) leave
3. you have met

4. alarm will ring
5. tire is
6. (it) (is)
7. (you) climb
8. Alex did quit
9. (you) bring
10. deer are
11. anyone can read
12. (you) abandon
13. floor could be
14. you were
15. (you) come
16. Dad is
17. I will visit
18. (it) (is)
19. (you) do speak
20. you have got

Exercise 5
1. 4
2. 1
3. 5
4. 2
5. 1
6. 3
7. 5
8. 1
9. 3
10. 2
11. 3
12. 5
13. 1
14. 4
15. 5

Exercise 6
1. 2
2. 2
3. 1
4. 3
5. 1
6. 1
7. 3

8. 5
9. 1
10. 4

Exercise 7
1. class
2. Colleen; typist
3. Liza Minelli; star
4. preacher; woman
5. soldiers; heroes
6. deadline; Tuesday
7. Goldie
8. problem; mosquitoes
9. penny; penny
10. smoke detector
11. movie; comedy
12. Janice; cook
13. college
14. spice; ginger
15. people; experts
16. dogs; hunters
17. Greta; actress
18. Sharla
19. weather; surprise
20. sound; wind

Exercise 8
1. hatchback; room; packages
2. basement; switch; ones; rest; house
3. Edith
4. freak; nature
5. screens; guests; gathering
6. president; company
7. stove
8. city; Jane Byrne; lakefront
9. Senator; Massachusetts; presidency; future
10. food; menu; restaurants
11. niece
12. drawer; cashier
13. Apollo; morning
14. dresser
15. *Madame Bovary*; art

ANSWER KEY (continued)

Exercise 9

1. secretary; joke
2. Betsy; flowers
3. senior citizens
4. riots
5. customer; package
6. strawberries
7. audience; trick
8. warning
9. Jerry; ladder
10. people; karate
11. minors; liquor
12. candy
13. courage
14. boys; discount
15. stores; business

Exercise 10

1. 1
2. 3
3. 6
4. 5
5. 4
6. 2
7. 2
8. 4
9. 3
10. 6
11. 5
12. 4
13. 1
14. 2
15. 5
16. 4
17. 3
18. 6
19. 5
20. 1

Exercise 11

1. 5
2. 3
3. 5
4. 2
5. 4
6. 3
7. 5
8. 2
9. 5
10. 4

Exercise 12

1. 5
2. 2
3. 4
4. 1
5. 5
6. 3
7. 4
8. 5
9. 2
10. 5
11. 3
12. 5
13. 5

Exercise 13

1. 5
2. 5
3. 2
4. 1
5. 1
6. 2
7. 3
8. 4

Exercise 14

1. 3
2. 3
3. 5
4. 2
5. 2
6. 3
7. 5
8. 4
9. 5
10. 1
11. 3
12. 4
13. 2
14. 3
15. 1
16. 2
17. 5
18. 1
19. 2
20. 5

Exercise 15

1. correct
2. bus's
3. landlord's
4. miners'
5. weeks'
6. correct
7. protesters'
8. Dr. Jones's
9. correct
10. people's
11. correct
12. correct
13. workers'
14. Mr. Gross's
15. correct

Exercise 16

1. These kinds of onions taste sweet.
2. correct
3. How many problems can one family have?
4. The boss assigned a large amount of work to me.
5. That type of child is fun to be around.
6. Can these types of holes be plugged up?
7. Those kinds of insects don't sting.

Exercise 17

1. practicing—object of preposition
2. speaking—simple subject
3. accounting—direct object
4. Tampering—simple subject
5. hiking—predicate nominative
6. parking—object of preposition
7. Drinking; driving—simple subject
8. shouting—direct object
9. golfing—appositive
10. dancing—direct object
11. ironing—direct object
12. Burping—simple subject
13. spitting—direct object
14. bookkeeping—appositive
15. embezzling—object of preposition

Exercise 18

1. Jose's fixing his car made a lot of noise.
2. David's walking in the snow left deep tracks.
3. correct
4. The children's laughing brightened my mood.
5. Make room on the table for Grandma's sewing.
6. Dad's cooking is a joke.
7. Everyone complained about Marie's washing the floor with a dirty mop.
8. We listened carefully to the coach's calling the plays.
9. The boat's rocking makes many people feel ill.
10. I wish someone could stop the baby's crying.
11. The television's playing so loud distracts me.
12. Your salting your food is not healthy.
13. A person's dreaming tells a lot about him.
14. correct
15. The shutter's flopping frightened the children.
16. Debbie's calling me made me lose my train of thought.
17. Willie's playing the drums always attracts an audience.
18. Your cutting your own hair was a disaster!
19. My wearing new shoes usually means blisters on my feet.
20. Ellen's drinking coffee keeps her awake at night.

Exercise 19

1. 1
2. 1
3. 5
4. 3
5. 2
6. 1
7. 2
8. 1
9. 5
10. 4
11. 1
12. 1
13. 2
14. 4
15. 2
16. 1
17. 3
18. 4
19. 5
20. 1
21. 4
22. 1
23. 3
24. 2
25. 3

Exercise 20

1. stirred
2. will be
3. Has reported
4. slips; will break
5. became
6. will decide
7. left; felt
8. is called
9. give
10. dimmed; booed
11. can sleep; needs
12. pour; cause
13. is; relieves
14. saw; hit
15. slams; jumps
16. has been
17. spread
18. must write
19. snapped
20. has been

Exercise 21

1. threw
2. wrote
3. understood
4. ran
5. slept
6. struck
7. fought
8. swam
9. caught
10. flew
11. stole
12. was
13. said
14. lost
15. felt
16. bit
17. saw
18. ate
19. took
20. taught

Exercise 22

1. eaten
2. seen
3. go
4. wrote
5. written
6. lit
7. felt
8. spoken
9. hurt
10. heard
11. gotten
12. broken
13. slept
14. left
15. frozen
16. wash
17. drinks
18. swept
19. known
20. think
21. slips
22. bought
23. answering
24. went
25. brushed
26. like
27. sat
28. order
29. took
30. trying

Exercise 23

1. 1
2. 2
3. 1
4. 5
5. 1
6. 3
7. 3
8. 3
9. 3
10. 3
11. 1
12. 1
13. 4
14. 3
15. 2
16. 3
17. 5
18. 1
19. 2
20. 1

ANSWER KEY (continued)

Exercise 24
1. shade
2. need
3. is
4. like
5. drinks
6. are
7. buy
8. were
9. have
10. are
11. have
12. swarm
13. curls
14. charge
15. meet
16. overstay
17. are
18. were
19. take
20. cause

Exercise 25
1. doesn't
2. is
3. makes
4. was
5. are
6. are
7. are
8. cost
9. were
10. don't
11. were
12. have
13. don't
14. don't
15. doesn't

Exercise 26
1. is
2. rub
3. grow
4. were; were
5. has
6. wasn't
7. need
8. live
9. goes
10. fill
11. leave
12. puts
13. were

14. comes
15. come

Exercise 27
1. was
2. was
3. was
4. likes
5. has
6. is
7. has
8. wasn't
9. Is
10. come
11. look
12. are
13. develop
14. causes
15. seems

Exercise 28
1. is
2. uses
3. come
4. helps
5. sign
6. looks
7. is
8. goes
9. calls
10. has
11. wears
12. is
13. receive
14. gets
15. comes

Exercise 29
1. grow
2. keep
3. shakes
4. is
5. are
6. is
7. leaves
8. are
9. uses
10. are
11. are
12. know
13. are
14. has
15. is

Exercise 30
1. don't
2. has
3. was
4. doesn't
5. were
6. is
7. is
8. was
9. were
10. inspects
11. hasn't
12. doesn't
13. eats
14. make
15. need
16. has
17. comes
18. grow
19. is
20. sound
21. gives
22. adds
23. sell
24. looks
25. are
26. are
27. doesn't
28. Weren't
29. entertain
30. come

Exercise 31
1. us
2. Our
3. your
4. they
5. her
6. himself
7. yourself
8. me
9. I
10. you
11. themselves
12. ours
13. she
14. We
15. us
16. him
17. themselves
18. theirs
19. her
20. he

Exercise 32

1. who
2. I
3. Whom
4. whoever
5. who
6. who
7. whom; who
8. We; they
9. they
10. whomever
11. He
12. Whom
13. whoever
14. who
15. Who

Exercise 33

1. I
2. she
3. them
4. me
5. me
6. he
7. him
8. we
9. him
10. she
11. we
12. we
13. he; she
14. he
15. she
16. he
17. I
18. he
19. me
20. I

Exercise 34

1. Your
2. I
3. my
4. We
5. us
6. my
7. I
8. we
9. your
10. Your

11. We
12. us
13. you
14. We
15. us
16. he
17. Your; me
18. We
19. We
20. you

Exercise 35

1. their
2. his
3. its
4. its
5. their
6. their
7. its
8. their
9. their
10. their
11. their
12. their

Exercise 36

1. that
2. his
3. which
4. who; her
5. his
6. which
7. that
8. his
9. whom
10. which
11. her
12. that
13. his
14. which
15. which

Exercise 37

1. 1
2. 2
3. 4
4. 1
5. 3
6. 5
7. 1

8. 2
9. 1
10. 1
11. 3
12. 5
13. 2
14. 2
15. 4
16. 5
17. 2
18. 1
19. 1
20. 5
21. 5
22. 2
23. 2
24. 4
25. 1

Exercise 38

1. adverb; stylish
2. adjective; flowers
3. adjective; blanket
4. adjective; cereal
5. adverb; scraped
6. adjective; peanuts
7. adverb; crept
8. adverb; come
9. adverb; go
10. adjective; movies
11. adverb; finished
12. adjective; water
13. adjective; person
14. adverb; sorry
15. adverb; frightened

Exercise 39

1. heartily
2. gently
3. tearful
4. poorly
5. romantic
6. quickly
7. real
8. Squeakily
9. wearily
10. loud
11. quiet
12. basic
13. hard
14. late

ANSWER KEY (continued)

Exercise 40

1. good
2. awful
3. badly
4. sore
5. well
6. noisy
7. well
8. easy
9. beautiful
10. good
11. strong
12. nervous
13. well
14. good
15. well
16. dirty
17. familiar
18. ready
19. well
20. short
21. eager
22. well
23. dull
24. proud
25. warm
26. sour
27. good
28. sick
29. bad
30. good

Exercise 41

1. 1
2. 1
3. 5
4. 3
5. 3
6. 2
7. 4
8. 1
9. 3
10. 2
11. 4
12. 2
13. 3
14. 5
15. 5

Exercise 42

1. smallest
2. harder
3. more beautifully
4. queerest
5. more patient
6. deepest
7. loudest
8. most popular
9. more eager
10. rainiest
11. happiest
12. longer
13. sloppiest
14. sicker
15. more silently

Exercise 43

1. worse
2. hungriest
3. further
4. hottest
5. most
6. uglier
7. most gently
8. curliest
9. heavier
10. easiest
11. tallest
12. deeper
13. fewer
14. most carefully
15. better
16. latest
17. farther
18. poorest
19. rainier
20. more uneven

Exercise 44

1. 1
2. 5
3. 1
4. 1
5. 3
6. 4
7. 3
8. 2
9. 3
10. 2
11. 5
12. 2
13. 1
14. 4
15. 2